C000142862

HARDPRESS.NET
HOME OF HARD-TO-FIND BOOKS

Advance Thought
by Charles E. Glass

Copyright © 2019 by HardPress

Address:
HardPress
8345 NW 66TH ST #2561
MIAMI FL 33166-2626
USA
Email: info@hardpress.net

WIDENER

HN R4AA 5

14465

hil 7054.114

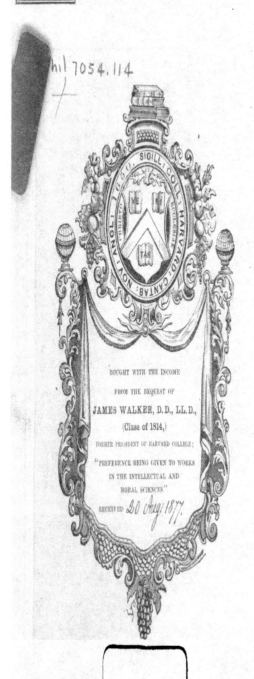

BOUGHT WITH THE INCOME

FROM THE BEQUEST OF

JAMES WALKER, D.D., LL.D.,

(Class of 1814,)

FORMER PRESIDENT OF HARVARD COLLEGE;

"PREFERENCE BEING GIVEN TO WORKS

IN THE INTELLECTUAL AND

MORAL SCIENCES"

RECEIVED 20 Aug: 1877.

ADVANCE THOUGHT.

PRINTED BY BALLANTYNE, HANSON AND CO.
EDINBURGH AND LONDON

ADVANCE THOUGHT.

BY

CHAS. E. GLASS.

LONDON:

TRÜBNER & CO., LUDGATE HILL.

1876.

[All rights reserved.]

Phil 7054.114

1877, Aug. 20.
Walker Fund.

PREFACE.

——◆——

In presenting this work it may be mentioned that it was originally commenced, simply as an effort of individual mind to explore the truth for itself, without any intention of bookmaking, and the printing of it was an afterthought. The writer did not believe that any peculiar gift, denied to others, was possessed by those through whom we have received inspired Scripture, as he held that inspiration, if admitted at all, must be regarded as the common inheritance of mankind; and that, as a necessity of increased enlightenment, it must even grow more generally open than it has yet been. [" It is written . . . they shall be all taught of God."] Perplexed between the unsatisfying dogmas of sectarianism, based chiefly upon " the letter that killeth," his desire was that his mind might be so enlightened as to realise " in spirit " such a knowledge of the Divine laws, as to find a religion in which he could have confidence. Whilst encouraged by an innate belief in an All-wise God—the evidences of whose governing mind are found in unalterable nature—and by a belief in ever open revelation, based upon circumstances which fell under his own personal experience in pursuing the inquiry as to religion and truth, he endeavoured to disabuse his mind of preconceived impressions of early religious teachings, and to draw by constant, earnest, and pure desire, the Divine light sought for, into an open, unprejudiced, and willing mind. ["Ask, and ye shall receive; knock, and it shall be opened unto you."]

This work, then, is not the result of book learning; but what is good of it is the gift of inspiration, although there are a few speculative deductions, presented as such; and there are quotations and extracts from received authorities, which have been added since the work was written, in order to strengthen, if possible, the conclusions arrived at, in the minds of some readers, who may require evidence of that nature. The writer makes no pretension to great literary ability in this work, and if readers want fine language, quotations from deep scientific authorities, or a profound knowledge of books, they can get plenty of that elsewhere. This book does not profess to furnish anything of the kind, but rests more particularly upon revelation, which, if pure, should be able to withstand any philosophical or scientific tests which may be brought forward to disprove it. It is maintained that, if readers will carefully endeavour to follow the meaning conveyed in these pages, they cannot fail to see a certain vein of consistent reasoning throughout, which may not only be instructive, but satisfying to their religious scruples. There are many points which would bear a better finish, in order that the tenor of the whole work be better understood, but there are many points which are extremely clear, and which, on the whole, must suffice to convey a good general impression to the mind. Whether or not there are those who will question the statement which attributes the ideas herein propounded to inspiration is of very little moment, as all statements must rely upon the truth contained in them for their vitality. It is felt that some will be greatly benefited by reading this book, otherwise the responsibility of making it public would not have been undertaken. At the same time, it is also felt that there are thousands whose minds are not prepared to receive the truths it contains, and to them it must, for the present, be as a "sealed book."

"The whole world," says the great minded Carlyle, "calls for new work and nobleness. Subdue mutiny, discord, widespread despair, by manfulness, justice, mercy, and wisdom. Chaos is dark, deep as hell; let light be, and there is instead a green, flowery world. Ob, it is great, and there is no other greatness! To make some nook of God's creation a little fruitfuller, better, more worthy of God! to make some human hearts a little wiser, manfuller, happier, more blessed, less accursed! It is work for a God! Sooty hell of mutiny, and savagery, and despair, can, by man's energy, be made a kind of heaven; cleared of its soot, of its mutiny, of its need to mutiny; the everlasting arch of heaven's azure overspanning *it* too, and its cunning mechanisms and tall chimney-steeples, as a birth of heaven; God and all men looking on it well pleased."

Let those who read and doubt, not rest satisfied, but appeal for themselves to the same source of unerring wisdom, and then abide the result. If Divine enlightenment and a knowledge of higher truths are looked for, they must be earnestly desired. There are many anxiously groping after truth who may not have the same opportunities of inquiry as the writer, and he presents this work because he holds that the increased intelligence of the age requires a religion which it can feel to be an actuality, and which it can reconcile with reason and the knowledge it has gained of the operation of the laws which govern the universe.

Sir Humphrey Davy has remarked :—

" If I could choose what would be most delightful, and I believe most useful to me, I should prefer a firm, religious belief to every other blessing ; for it makes life a discipline of goodness—creates new hopes when all earthly hopes vanish ; and throws over the decay, the destruction of existence, the most gorgeous of all lights ; awakens life even in death, and from corruption and decay calls up beauty and divinity ; makes an instrument of torture and of shame the ladder of ascent to paradise ; and far above all combinations of earthly hopes, calls up the most delightful visions of plains and amaranths, the gardens of the blest, the security of everlasting joys, where the sensualist and the sceptic view only gloom, decay, annihilation, and despair."

Intelligent thinkers and inquirers have lost all sympathy for sectarian distinctions, as tending to alienate people instead of cultivating brotherly love and unity ; and they turn from the teachings of theology, as presenting an inadequately high and pure conception of divinity. In all ages—according to fixed natural laws—it is held that man has, by inspiration, received forms of religion suited to his capacity of intellect ;

and, at the present time, the strong exercise of pure and fervent desire for truth, which is so noticeable in certain quarters, will undoubtedly attract to him a religion in which he will find confidence, consolation, and hope.

" Books," remarked Lord Dudley, " are loved by some merely as elegant combinations of thought ; by others, as a means of exercising the intellect. By some they are considered as the engines by which to propagate opinions ; and by others they are only deemed worthy of serious regard when they constitute repositories of matters of fact. But perhaps the most important use of literature has been pointed out by those who consider it as a record of the respective modes of moral and intellectual existence that have prevailed in successive ages, and who value literary performances in proportion as they preserve a memorial of the spirit which was at work in real life during the times when they were written."

CONTENTS.

CONTENTS.

c

ADVANCE THOUGHT.

INTRODUCTORY CHAPTER.

WHY should any one brought up in the established faiths of the day seek to examine into and prove the fitness of the doctrines inculcated by the ministers of religion? To the unprejudiced seeker after higher truths there are many reasons which may be advanced to establish the reasonableness and necessity of such an examination. The most important of these, perhaps, rests upon the fact of man being endowed with certain reasoning powers, the proper exercise of which is regarded as the highest object of his existence, and the neglect to use which is regarded as most debasing. If man had ever been contented to receive as conclusive truth all that had been written or spoken by his predecessors, and to copy all courses and things which had been shapen by those before him, resting under the conviction that no higher truths could be attained and no better means devised, there would not have been any such thing as improvement or progression. The resources of this beautiful world would be unknown and unused—arts, manufactures, mines, and commerce would not have any existence—social intercourse and civilised government would be unknown—and people would be congregated in dense masses, too unhealthy to live without pestilence and famine being constantly with them, while the greater part of the habitable world would be unexplored.

> " What is a man,
> If his chief good, and market of his time,
> Be but to sleep and feed ? a beast, no more.

A

Sure, he that made us with such large discourse,
Looking before, and after, gave us not
That capability and godlike reason
To fust in us unus'd."—*Hamlet.*

Tradition, custom, precedent, and fashion should be gauged
by their fitness to things present, and should not be tolerated when upheld to nurse ignorance, assist oppression, or
pamper sterile impotency. As Southey very truly remarks :—

"It is not for man to rest in absolute contentment. He is
born to hopes and aspirations, as the sparks fly upwards, unless
he has brutified his nature, and quenched the spirit of immortality which is his portion."

What ! are we to be told that we are not to be benefited
by a careful examination into the laws governing the universe ? Is the captain of that fine ship, crowded with
emigrants full of hope, starting on a voyage to the antipodes, to be advised to throw those charts of his overboard
which show the hidden rocks of mid-ocean, the course of
the winds, and the ocean currents ? and is he to be told
to send after those charts his compass, astronomical tables,
sextant, chronometer, barometer, and log, because, forsooth,
these were not used in Scripture times ? If such vast good
and material happiness have been gained by the study of
our material world,—if it has led to the peopling of lands
before unexplored, and has converted the ocean into a comparatively safe highway between people living all over the
habitable world,—are we to be told that the laws governing
our eternal welfare are to be neglected, unexplored, or not
examined into according to the best means at our disposal ?

All advancement attained at the present time must be
credited to those who, having a correct appreciation of their
responsibility for the proper use of the talents with which
they were endowed, had a desire for something better, or,
wishing for gain of some kind, manfully endeavoured to
"prove all things," and to hold to that which, in their best
judgment with experience, was found best. When man is
brought to feel that he must "bear his own burthen," he
exerts himself in a becoming manner, and the mind which
is exerted soon discovers that the pursuit of worldly happiness by the acquisition of wealth and distinction, for the
gratification merely of selfish, sensual, or material instincts,
is foolishness, as these are unsatisfying to the few who

succeed in acquiring them; whilst such happiness, even were it attainable, must necessarily be unprofitable, as it would be transient as the material form whose fleeting tastes they are designed to pander to. The inquiring mind once able fully to realise that true happiness can alone be attained by the cultivation of the unselfish spiritual nature which decays not with the body, if true to itself, will seek for and endeavour to attain a greater knowledge of the laws of God, and higher conceptions of deity, to meet the growing requirements of its better nature; and it will not rest satisfied with the pursuit of mere worldly gain, but will earnestly examine into the sufficiency of the superstructure upon which its religious beliefs or its hopes in eternity are grounded, and refuse to accept, unquestioned, the dicta of any one else upon a matter of such infinite importance to itself. The difficulties which present themselves in the way of any one setting out upon such a course, it must be acknowledged, are very great and trying; and if wanting in lasting earnestness, the inquirer soon lapses into the fashionable condition of chronic indifference to all things, except to such as are connected with the gratification of the material tastes, and so falls out of the ranks of the persevering few to swell still more the world's throng. If the inquirer appeals to professional religious teachers, he finds them expounding different systems of sin and redemption, according to their respective creeds,—all their systems being based upon the same authority. Between Protestants and Roman Catholics, for instance, the inquirer finds the former section professing that each individual should study the Bible and draw his own conclusions for himself, yet that they mostly neglect to do so—he finds, in short, a "Protestantism which has ceased to protest;" and he finds the Roman Catholic section professing the ability alone in their priests to understand aright that authority, and so practically acknowledging that they have themselves no duty in any inquiry into the plans of salvation propounded by their priests. It is a phase of human nature, that when the mind realises a higher form of truth, susceptible of being expressed in a wider, different light, or in terms different from that in which it has been propounded hitherto, a conclusion is immediately jumped at, that the previous conviction did not contain truth in any form whatever, and that the new form of

truth is truth in its very highest form, or in perfection.
[See " Divergence of Thought," conclusions upon the words
" Might is right " in another part of this book.]   Each party
naturally accepts that form which appeals most to its reason,
and for this cause the minds of each honestly see good in
their own convictions, and inferior good or bad in the
opinions accepted by the other party.   A higher form of
truth will therefore probably be found elsewhere ; and
while Protestants may learn with advantage — education
notwithstanding—that only those minds which sincerely
desire divine enlightenment in the paths of spiritual thought
can realise the higher truths which are to be found in
inspired Scripture, the Roman Catholics may also learn
that spiritual enlightenment is open to the most humble
citizen, be he layman or priest, and that religious orders
are no passport either to what is called heaven or to infal-
libility.

Confusing and difficult as religion or the cultivation
of the spiritual nature has been made by theology and
the inventions and machinations of man, the earnest seeker
for truth may soon have his paths of thought made straight,
and realise with heartfelt gratitude that God is ever near
the pure in heart, irrespective altogether of religious systems and dogmas, and that instead of these being essential to salvation, they should be held altogether subordinate
thereto.   The religious beliefs of Christendom are based
upon the general admission that certain men were divinely
inspired to write the Bible.   All agree in the belief that, by
a certain process in nature in times past, men who earnestly
sought truth had it revealed to them by inspiration.   Why,
then, should they not hold to this belief, and apply it to
their own present time and their own particular case, and
seek to obtain spiritual truth by revelation precisely in the
same way and from the same source as in times past ?   Have
the processes of nature been altered ?   There does not
appear to be any tangible reason to advance why people
should not now make use of revelation.   Is not prayer at
the present time answered ? and are not some men even
now inspired as in times past ?   What are the guides given
to us to ascertain whether the deliverances of men who, in
our own day, are at times the vehicles of inspired sayings,
are divine or erroneous ?   Have we not reasoning powers

given to us for use ? and do we not find in nature surrounding us certain immutable laws indicating the unerring authorship of the divine mind ? If natural laws could be suspended or altered, that would show them to be imperfect and faulty, and like those of man, which ever require to be altered as he grows wiser and better ; and God might be charged with teaching falsehood and deception. But such is not the case, for nature by its unaltering precision teaches us TRUTH above all things, as by its bounteous administrations to the necessities of all creatures it also teaches us LOVE as another leading principle of existence. If the laws of nature are perfect, as they must necessarily be, are they not unerring guides ? Milton remarks that, " In contemplation of created things, by steps we may ascend to God ; " Goethe says of nature that it is " The living, visible garment of God ; " and Carlyle speaks of it as " The time-vesture of God, that reveals Him to the wise and hides Him from the foolish." Any theories of sin or redemption, based upon dogmatic assertion, or upon the writings of men who have been mediums of otherwise pure inspiration, which do not agree with the divine light which any earnest man may obtain through himself, and which further do not agree with the unalterable laws of nature, must be cast aside from the mind as worse than useless. The Bible, as we have it, is full of highly inspired lessons ; yet, notwithstanding this, and the circumstance of its being the generally accepted authority of Christian sects, we should not receive anything in it which clashes with " The spirit of truth " within us. The persevering inquirer will soon get to regard it in its correct form, and discover that the biblical writings are now received in a different light from what they were originally regarded, and from what they were intended to be regarded.

The writers of the various books were not party to the after-thought of the Churches by which these writings were collected in the form now called the Bible. In most instances the writers were unknown—they were not consulted as to whether their writings should be so presented to the world, nor as to whether they themselves believed these writings to be truly inspired ; and although religious teachers now delight to represent the Bible as wholly the veritable "Word of God," no such claim was originally held by the Churches by whom the books of the New Testament were collected, nor by the writers who penned them, and there were some who did not believe in their inspiration when the Churches were considering the introduction of certain books. Each one must accept that which he finds nourishing to his higher spiritual nature, and reject that which is debasing, whether it be found in the teachings of the Bible, in the lessons of any one, be he ever so wise, or in the daily experiences of life. The writer, of his own experience, knows [see " Personal Experiences " at end of this book] that inspiration is now as much a fact as it has been in the past, and he believes there are men who now use it as much; if not more, than did the scribes of the Bible. So far as his own experience is concerned, he feels it due to say here that although he has had revealed to him by impression or inspiration, word by word, whole pages of information that was not within his recollection of previous knowledge, and although he has been careful not to sit down to write without first well observing the conditions in nature by which he believes pure inspiration may be expected, he would no more think of asking his readers to accept unchallenged his pennings than he would himself accept the account of creation which represents the world and all therein to have been made within six days—no more than he would believe that God, after creating the world in six days, was fatigued and therefore rested upon the seventh day, and that He instituted Sabbath observance because that He himself had required one day's rest after six days' labour—no more than he can believe that the sun and moon stood still at the command of Joshua in order that he might slay the Amorites—no more than he believes the New Testament writers where they claim that our beloved Jesus of Nazareth was in truth God himself, when Jesus, prophetically guarding against this doctrine, point-blank disclaimed to bear witness of himself—and no more than he can believe that sin came into the world because that Satan, literally as a serpent, led Eve and Adam to eat of certain fruit, or that Satan as a materialised person led Jesus up to a mountain high enough to show him " all the kingdoms of the earth," and offered them to him if he would worship him.

" I can of mine own self do nothing : as I hear, I judge : and my judgment is just ; because I seek not mine own will, but the will of the Father which hath sent me. If I bear witness of myself, my witness is not true."—John v. 30, 31.

" Why callest thou me good ? there is none good but one, that is, God."—Mark x. 18.

" No man can come to me, except the Father, which hath sent me, draw him. . . . . I came not to do mine own will, but the will of Him that sent me."—John vi. 44, 38.

" I speak to the world those things which I have heard of Him. . . . . Ye shall know that I do nothing of myself ; but as my Father hath taught me, I speak these things. . . . . The Father hath not left me alone ; for I do always those things that please Him."—John viii. 26, 28, 29.

" It is written in the prophets, And they shall be all taught of God. Every man therefore that hath heard, and hath learned of the Father, cometh unto me."—John vi. 45.

In our times, the reliability of the utterances of men are weighed by the intrinsic worth which they may be found to have, and if offered by any one as on the authority of some reliable source, the known character and trustworthiness of the scribe or messenger is duly weighed. So far as Scriptural representations are concerned, these tests are utterly ignored. The effect is, that were any writers in our time to offer a work containing anything like the same utterly absurd and God-dishonouring statements, they would, from the mere want of that traditionary power, backed up by priestcraft and superstition, which the Scriptures enjoy, be scouted, notwithstanding the great beauty and truth of many parts, as wicked, immoral, and unworthy of reading. Take the character and pretensions of Moses, whose commissions, like those of most of the other great lights of the Old Testament, are usually introduced with the words, "Thus saith the Lord." Moses, it is recorded, murdered an Egyptian and hid his body in the sand, and finding that the deed had been discovered, and that he was to be executed for it, he fled into another country, where, by representing himself as divinely commissioned to deliver the Hebrews from bondage, and getting his brother to join him in this enterprise, he tells them, as from God, that they are not to go away empty, but that all the women are to " borrow " of their neighbours jewels and raiment. This low type of character, presented to us in that of the great lawgiver, is not peculiar to him, but may be found in most of the leading men of the Old Testament. Yet it is inspiration through such channels we are asked to accept in place of present inspiration, suited to our own time and circumstances. It is simply a violation and debasement of the reasoning powers which God has given to us, to receive, in our day, all Scriptural presentations as literally true.

It is related of one of the most talented functionaries of the Roman Catholic Church, that, when he was recently interrogated by a distinguished chemist as to the killing of Abel, he replied that had Cain—who, as a city-builder, is the representative of progressive civilisation—not killed Abel—who is the representative of the pastoral pursuits—there would not have been any progression ; and that it was in the nature of things that the pastoral should give way before the advancing interests of civilisation. This little incident shows that some of the advanced minds of our day can see something beyond the superficial literal meanings in many Scriptural passages which are usually read without thought.

"Beware," said Bishop Sanderson, "of misapplying Scripture. It is a thing easily done, but not so easily answered. I know not any one gap that hath let in more dangerous errors into the Church than this,—that men take the words of the text, fitted to particular occasions, and to the condition of the times wherein they were written, and then apply them to themselves and others as they find them, without due respect had to the differences that may be between those times and cases and the present."

We may approve of the establishment of a custom by which—the Sabbath being, as Jesus taught, "made for man"—as many people as possible may be brought to the cultivation of their higher spiritual nature and the recruiting of their physical powers, by the setting apart of one day or as many days in the week as they can be induced to observe. In the God-like manner in which Jesus is represented to have met the temptations of "Satan," we may recognise the ease with which one of the inspiration and power to which he had attained might have grasped earthly riches and position had he so chosen, and we may understand the greatness of the trial and temptation which the vivid knowledge of this must have had upon one "who had not where to rest his head," had he selected to abandon his high mission for so called worldly happiness. And in the quotation in reply which Jesus is represented to have given when challenged to throw himself from a pinnacle of the temple in proof that he was divinely cared for and could not be injured—" Thou shalt not tempt the Lord thy God "—a wholesome lesson is furnished to the effect that, if we deliberately violate natural laws, we must not expect to be saved from the consequences by any especial interposition or a suspension of those laws. We may accept the blissful condition in which Adam is presented to us previous to " the fall," as a good prophetic figure of what man may yet rise to in those later times when he shall hold communion with and "be taught of God ;" and we may also approve of the idea that our present spiritual blindness is mostly owing to the disregard of conscience or the still small voice within, which is ever counselling us to hold the animal propensities of our nature under subjection; but we cannot admit that the animal instincts should be regarded as a Satanic influence, for they are most undoubtedly essential and beneficial to our being, and reflect the infinite love and wisdom of God. We may even hold it to be unfair to estimate the true character of Moses, and some other prominent men that are presented to us in Bible history, by the standards of modern thought, inasmuch as they lived under vastly different influences and circumstances. A good authority reminds us that—

" It behoves us always to bear in mind, that while actions are always to be judged by the immutable standard of right and wrong, the judgments which we pass upon men must be qualified by considerations of age, country, station, and other accidental circumstances ; and it will then be found that he who is most charitable in his judgment is generally the least unjust."

Another authority, Bishop Hall, remarks that—

" There is no word or action but may be taken either with the right hand of charitable construction, or the sinister interpretation of malice and suspicion ; and all things succeed as they are taken. To construe an evil action well," says he, " is but a pleasing deceit to myself ; but to misconstrue a good thing is a treble wrong—to myself, the action, and the author."

Of Moses, as he is represented, it may be said, then, that he was in his time a born leader of his people. The Hebrews were in bondage, and his parents, no doubt smarting under Pharaoh's yoke, longed for the deliverance of themselves and kindred; and the strong mental influence thus exerted by his parents by natural law attracted, it may reasonably be inferred, to their offspring that great mental character which distinguished Moses as a deliverer. Considering next those higher spiritual laws by which such minds are guarded over and guided, we may understand how it came about that he was brought up under all the advantages of education in religion, social laws, and rules of government, which were acquired under Pharaoh's roof to befit him for his career; and how it was brought about that he should be nursed by his own mother, who would whisper in his ear the tale of his parentage, and tell him of the longings of his countrymen for deliverance, and thus fan his nature aflame. ["Take heed that ye despise not one of these little ones : for . . . . their angels do always behold the face of my Father which is in heaven."—Matt. xviii. 10. And thus the destinies of the infant Moses, too, were no doubt watched over.] The maternal influences upon his nature become apparent in the account furnished of his siding with the Hebrew ; and, indeed, throughout the whole of his after-life, Moses, in his time, may very fairly, perhaps, be regarded as the born saviour of his people, and his influence was no doubt beneficial to their then condition, although in our time he would not be tolerated ; for mind is now more susceptible of realising those higher spiritual truths which could only in his time be prefigured by crude material forms and symbols, the observance of which had to be enforced with severe penalties. [" Many prophets and righteous men have desired to see those things which ye see, and have not seen them," &c.—Matt. xiii. 17. "The law and the prophets were until John : since that time the kingdom of God is preached."—Luke xvi. 16.] In the third chapter of Ephesians Paul says—

" How that by revelation he made known unto me the mysteries, whereby, when ye read, ye may understand, ... which in other ages was not made known unto the sons of men, as it is now revealed, . . . to the intent that now . . . . might be made known . . . . the wisdom of God ; . . . . that ye, being rooted and grounded in love, may be able to comprehend what is the breadth, and length, and depth, and height."

Before the cultivation of mind, and the study of natural laws and the history of the earth, man could not realise the same high conceptions of Deity ; allowances must therefore be made for the ridiculous accounts handed down to us of creation, &c.—of Joshua making the sun and moon to stand still—of the allurements of his Satanic majesty—and for a host of other absurd statements intermixed throughout the beautiful lessons of the Bible ; for it was not then suspected by the scribes that the supposition of the earth being flat would afterwards be disproved, nor was it then known that the revolution of the earth on its axis produced day and night ; and this shows us that earnest investigation in time brings out the higher truths. If all the expectations of man in the future as to his eternal happiness or misery are to rest—as the masses by uninvestigated tradition now slovenly suppose they should—upon certain theories of sin and redemption which are grounded upon the Bible, which is made up simply of certain writings of *fallible* men supposed to have been capable of *infallible* inspiration, the character of inspiration itself and the laws in nature by which it is received are surely worth consideration.

Herein lies the very key to a knowledge of good and evil, according to our capacities of reception. This key is within the reach of all, and without its use man's earthly career must be one of comparative non-progression, and be characterised by ignorance, with mental doubt and fear. The great error of the religions of our day consists in the want of a proper appreciation of the law of inspiration, and the consequent wholesale reception of pernicious doctrines which otherwise would be found unworthy of being considered divinely inspired. If it be generally received that men in the Old Testament times received by inspiration rules of life suited to their condition and circumstances, and that in the New Testament times, through Jesus, John, Peter, and others, were received, by the same means, higher rules of life suited to their then more enlightened condition ; if the old precepts, "An eye for an eye, and a tooth for a tooth," and "Love thy neighbour, and hate thine enemy," were, in the times of Jesus, altered to "Whosoever smites thee on thy right cheek, turn to him the other also," and "Love your enemies, bless them that curse you, do good to them that hate you," &c. ; and if both of these rules of life, diametrically opposed as they appear to be to each other, are received as divinely inspired truths, what is the inference but that rules of life may be obtained to answer our ever altering requirements by inspiration, according to the capacity of mind to receive ; and that it is the duty, as it is to the eternal welfare, of every one to strive earnestly after the highest conceptions of truth ?

Acting under this belief, there are many consistent Christians in our day who, while they accept all that is presented to them of the history and teachings of Jesus in the four Gospels which is found spiritually nourishing, do not necessarily accept all that is given, simply because it is found there. Even the Lord's Prayer, as given in Matt. vi., and which, by the way, does not terminate with the words "for Christ's sake," cannot be used by them for various reasons. For instance, the words " Our Father who art in heaven " to them are meaningless, as they believe God to be everywhere present, while they regard heaven to be a condition as much as a place. [John iii., " Except a man be born again he cannot see the kingdom of God. . . . We speak that we do know. . . . If I have told you of earthly things, and ye believe not, how shall ye believe, if I tell you of heavenly things ? . . . No man hath ascended up to heaven but he that came down from heaven, even the Son of man, who IS in heaven."] " Thy will be done in earth, as it is in heaven," has little significance to them ; for if " heaven " be looked upon as a condition of happiness, it is necessarily the will of God that all should enjoy it when they are capable of doing so. " Give us this day our daily bread, and forgive us our debts, as we forgive our debtors," they contend that God sends His sunshine and rain, and daily bread also, alike to the good and less good of His creatures, be they ever so insignificant,—that it is irreverent to bring God to our own level by supposing it possible that we should be able to forgive others according to the love which we seek, and which distinguishes His nature ; and that it is ridiculous to suppose that we only require the same measure from Him that we measure out to others. " Lead us not into temptation," these words they hold to be highly dishonouring, as they give a Satanic character to the Supreme Being, inasmuch as they imply that God is in the habit of specially leading us astray, and that by the asking He may be dissuaded from doing so. What we may ask for is that wisdom and strength be given, by natural law, to enable us to appreciate and overcome the many trials which are essential to our spiritual welfare ; that we may be surrounded by pure and godlike influences, at all times attracted to us by the purity and sincerity of our desires ; that we may realise the weak points in our own characters, and learn to pray for, or earnestly desire, those things only which are for the general good ; that every secret thought and purpose of our mind at their inception be carefully analysed by conscience, to see if they conform to the will of God, so that our higher spiritual natures may thereby attain the ascendancy and keep in subjection our material natures ; that we may live in harmony with the laws of nature, and faithfully perform that part which we may believe to be assigned to us individually in the great scheme of God's beautiful universe ; and that we may be kept nourished by that " manna from heaven." that " meat " which Jesus alluded to at the well (a magnetic current of divine impression and communion), which shall guide us as a pillar of cloud and fire through this trackless wilderness towards the promised land.

The enlightenment of mind which is obtained by inspiration has in all times represented one of the most powerful agencies towards human happiness and progress ; yet, since the days of the youthful unlettered Jesus of Nazareth, who astonished the doctors in the Temple by his sayings, and more particularly since printing, it has been comparatively unused. People acknowledge the power of the inspirational teachings received by other men, under other circumstances, for their own guidance, but they fail to realise that the same source of power is, in their own day, open to themselves for practical use, without there being any necessity whatever for constantly looking back upon the dead past, like " Lot's wife." The Christianity of the present time is but Christianity in name, and not in reality ; but we hopefully look for the dawn of a brighter day, when, with the dispersion of prevailing darkness, all may be brought to see more clearly the beauties to be disclosed by the Sun of righteousness.   *Pascal,* in speaking of true Christianity, says :—

"There are three means of believing—by inspiration, by reason, and by custom. Christianity does yet admit none for its sons who do not believe by inspiration. Nor does it injure reason or custom, or debar them of their proper force ; on the contrary, it directs us to open our minds by the proofs of the former, and to confirm our minds by the authority of the latter. But then it chiefly engages us to offer ourselves, with all humility, to the succours of inspired grace, which alone can produce the true and salutary effect."

Much of the purer matter and the better lessons of the Scriptures is contained in allegory and symbol, which can only be understood in its fuller meaning by the more spiritually enlightened. There is a kind of freemasonry about them ; and although the uninitiated may see these symbols and know their general use, the scope of thought which they call up will be vastly different, according to the conceptions of truth on the part of observers. Since man has neglected to use inspirational power in his pursuit of the higher truths of nature, and has mostly rested content with printed traditions for his spiritual nourishment, the more essential truths of his being have been well-nigh lost in his accumulations of musty rubbish, and the uncertain sounds which he obtains from symbols are now only as of "sounding brass or a tinkling cymbal." Since the eager pursuit of the higher truths and secrets of nature which the learned fathers of freemasonry strove hard to attain and to lecture upon to others, and since their precepts have been committed to paper to be learned by mere rote by members upon entering each degree, the so-called secrets or higher truths of freemasonry have also become things of the past, and there is left perhaps nothing but what might be taught in schools. Relieved of any moral responsibility, if any, which might attach to one of the craft, the inconvenience and risk of writing in the dark on such matters may only be compensated for on the ground that, if erroneous, they form no material part of the argument in this work.

It is submitted that the pursuit of divine truth, by the cultivation of the higher spiritual nature, lies very much in a channel of symbols which nature is everywhere unfolding to us for our edification, happiness, and enlightenment ;

and that—as in Freemasonry—no one can attain the higher degrees who has not been fully initiated into the lower ones.

When David, about three thousand years ago, used the following words, he appears to have had presented to him, as an instance of the power and scope of symbols, most advanced views as to the process by which mind expresses itself through matter, as it progresses from the lowest material forms to those higher combinations represented in the mind of enlightened man, that beautiful temple upon which no sound of hammer is heard in its construction : " My substance was not hid from Thee, when I was made in secret, and curiously wrought in the lowest parts of the earth. Thine eyes did see my substance, yet being imperfect ; and in Thy book were all my members written, which in continuance were fashioned when as yet there was none of them." John the Baptist expressed the same idea when he used the words, " I say unto you, that God is able of these stones to raise up children unto Abraham." Whether it be the building up to a thing of beauty and joy for ever of the world which is given us to reside upon, by all people exerting themselves for the greatest good and happiness of all, by making the most of the materials which surround them —whether it be the building of an individual mind or the building of a dwelling-house—in all these the symbols and lessons of life are to be learned ; and although the devices of man may be misleading, the book of nature contains no misstatements or misrepresentations.

Sala remarks—

" How beautifully is it ordered that, as many thousands work for one, so must every individual bring his labour to make the whole ! The highest is not to despise the lowest, nor the lowest to envy the highest ; each must live in all and by all. Who will not work, neither shall he eat. So God has ordered that men, being in need of each other, should learn to love each other, and bear each other's burthens."

The wise man will not build his house upon the sand. The master-mind is represented in the architect who designs, plans, and sees to the carrying out of the work, and in him rests the credit of the work, as mind is the source of all power ; yet, as mind to the material senses can only be communicated through the varied phases by which it expresses itself in the different forms of matter, the architect makes use of labourers according to their skill in order to carry out his design of satisfying the senses of those who may appreciate the work. There is work for all ; and even the hodman cannot be dispensed with, for he too contributes to the essential labour of the complete structure. The incongruous materials in sand, lime, bricks, and stone, which exhibit no adhesion or affinity for each other whilst laying about separately, and the occupations of the varied kinds of skilled and unskilled labour, which bear little or no resemblance in their operations to each other, and the varied interests and conditions of the human race, which appear so discordant, all by the direction of mind, possessing a knowledge of natural laws, are each and all transformed, in time, into a cemented, lasting, and beautiful whole. In the various branches, each one must begin at the A B C of his profession before he can become a master of it, and at each stage he must so apply himself as to become initiated into the use of the different tools of his craft. So is it with this beautiful universe or world, with its people of varied abilities and its wonderful resources, which are given to us to analyse and to employ our mind and labour upon in fashioning them, so as to render everything useful and beautiful—a very heaven for ourselves, to the everlasting glory of the Father, the truly great Architect of all. In every department of life, nature, by the symbols it unfolds in the laws governing matter and mind, will be found to be repeating itself, first in the lower, and then in the higher forms of being. Be he king or the meanest subject, in the daily occupation of his life, and in the materials, and even in the use of the tools at his disposal, if he be a seeker for truth, he may obtain that enlightenment which will afford him a just appreciation of God's loving designs, and lead him to entertain certain confidence and deep admiration as to their perfection. Whether man has regard to the manifold adjustments of disintegration and combination represented in the building of a world, or in the comparatively insignificant collection of materials used in the erection of a residence for himself, or whether he limits his observation even to the simple means by which a block of stone is quarried, dressed, and made fit for his building, the same wholesome natural laws may be disclosed to his mind. First, by way of figure, for instance, is represented the crude stone in the rock of ages. Second, the rudeness of the tools, and the uncultivated condition of the mind, which suffice to make an impression upon it. Third, the encouragement and reward which the perseverance of comparatively unskilled labour realises by the disintegration of the stone with the crowbar or slow movement of mind, or the happiness which great reforms bring, even when these are brought about by the steady drill of agitation of riper minds, leading to the explosive revolutionary blast which accomplishes the end in view, although moving with such awful suddenness the masses forward to their destiny in the midst of ruins. Fourth, the rough-hewing to reduce a stone, thus disintegrated, to proportions, to receive the after finer dressings, may be said to resemble the condition of worlds when signs of vegetation are first appearing, before they are ready for the reception of mind in the higher forms of animal life, or it may be taken to resemble the parental influences upon children before they are sent to school. Fifth, that stage in which the block passes through the hands of the ordinary masons, when the maul and chisel, directed with the sufficiency of power and skill of the workman, make it to yield to the square and rule of method and exactness by which the mason should gauge his every action, and by which the stone is to be made fit for the building—or, if it be suitable stone, it will pass through the hands of the sculptor, who, with more elaborate tools, records more of mind upon it, and prepares it for the ornamentation as well as usefulness of the building. Taken in another light, for " stones " we may read the " children " born to people, with whom it rests to shape their character to the best of their ability, in order that they may be fitted to take a proper place in the structure of society. Sixth, may be traced the properly-shapen block, like a young man who has just completed his education at school, and is about to enter the career of manhood, when his every movement must be tested by the plumb and line of conscientious thought to make it take a worthy part in the divine structure of natural laws under the great Architect, who requires the concerted and harmonious action of all the parts for the perfect building. It is doubtful whether any teacher has ever inculcated higher spiritual laws for the guidance of man than did Jesus, and

B

those lessons are notably drawn from the laws of nature,
and they are conveyed to us in symbols of higher and lower
meaning, according to the capacity of our minds to receive ;
yet, we do not hear of his writing epistles, or letters, or
sermons, or catechisms, or confessions of faith, nor of his
being a book-student, or otherwise being "coached up" for
the ministry by the study of languages and theology.
Scripture, although known to him, was not allowed to re-
strict his mind, for, soaring above and beyond its limits, he
boldly declared the magnificent lesson of his whole life,
when he uttered the words : " A new commandment I give
unto you, That ye love one another." Such was the power
of tradition in Scripture, and such the multiplicity of
doctrines drawn therefrom in Jesus' time even, that his
purer teachings were opposed most by priests and professing religionists, who, too, were his greatest persecutors.
Upon one occasion he is represented to have been asked by
the Pharisees and scribes how it was his disciples walked
not according to the tradition of the elders, when he replied : " Well hath Esaias prophesied of you, hypocrites—
This people honoureth me with their lips, but their heart
is far from me.   Howbeit in vain do they worship me,
teaching for doctrines the commandments of men. For,
laying aside the commandments of God, ye hold the tradition of men." The nation represented as " the chosen people
of God," through whom both Freemasonry and Scriptural
inspiration are supposed to be handed down, were so blinded
by trusting to tradition, and by the neglect on their parts
to search for spiritual light and to use inspiration for themselves, that the words " the stone which the builders rejected
has become the head of the corner," read like prophetic
Freemasonry, for truth is enduring, and the building of
the Church must progress, and many of the lessons and influences of Jesus in the work will yet be regarded in a
higher light, even by those professing Christians who now,
through a like trusting to tradition and dogma, are suffering very much under the same erroneous influences as were
the Jews when they crucified him. [1 Pet. ii. 5, " Ye also, as
living stones, are built up a spiritual house, a holy priesthood,
to offer up spiritual sacrifices, acceptable to God." 1 Cor. iii.,
" According to the grace of God, ... as a master-builder,
I have laid the foundation, and another buildeth thereon.

But let every man take heed how he buildeth thereon. . . . . Every man's work shall be manifest, ... and the fire" (the magnetic fire of conscious mind) "shall try every man's work of what sort it is. If any man's work abide, ... he shall receive a reward" (the conscious happiness of having done good). "If any man's work shall be burned" (all untruth which has been propagated is consumed in time, but the fires of conscience yield pain to the propagators in the process), "he shall suffer loss; but he himself shall be saved; yet so as by fire. Know ye not that ye are the temple of God, and that the Spirit of God dwelleth in you?"]

The foregoing lines of thought upon symbols of language and nature are intended to indicate the many everyday channels through which lessons of life may be gained by those who are really anxious. Instead of copying others, let man seek earnestly of the Father for that enlightenment of mind which substantially improves his eternal being, and at every turn he will realise divine impression, or original thought, suited to his requirements. Eph. i., "That . . . . the Father . . . . may give . . . . you the spirit of wisdom and revelation in the knowledge of him, ... that ye may know what is the hope." Those who desire wisdom and truth have a wholesome lesson before them in the dream to which Solomon owed his greatness. Solomon, on one occasion, before he had gained renown, was engaged in prayer and sacrifice (1 Kings iii.), and afterwards, while in sleep, he was impressed to ask God for what he most wished; and his mind having been previously filled with anxiety to know how best to perform his duty to God and the people over whom he had just been called to reign, he said, "Thou hast made me king, and I am but a little child, and know not how to go out or come in. Give therefore thy servant an understanding heart to judge the people that he may discern between good and bad;" and he was answered to the effect that because his desires were pure, and he had not asked, in selfishness, for long life, nor riches, nor the lives of his enemies, he would be given a wise and an understanding heart superior to any one. Solomon profited by that dream, for he acted up to it, and fully realised its teachings throughout his prosperous career; for in the 4th chapter we are told that Solomon's wis-

dom excelled that of all the children of the east country
and Egypt, and his fame was in all nations round about,
and " he spake three thousand proverbs, and his songs
were one thousand and five ; and he spake of trees,
from the cedar of Lebanon to the hyssop that springeth
out of the wall : also of beasts, fowl, creeping things,
and fishes, and there came of all people to hear of his
wisdom." Man's first duty is to make the best use
of his material senses for the common good. There is a
knowledge, however, which reaches far beyond the comparatively limited sphere of observation to which the material
senses of man are circumscribed, even when these are aided
by the keenest instruments invented, the manipulations
of the chemist, the investigations of science, and the deductions of logic ; and that knowledge is represented by
spiritual revelation, and that revelation, be it well known,
is now open to man to use. The actuality of prophecy by
revelation is well established. By prophecy is not meant
the mere predictions of man founded upon human observation and calculation—foretelling an effect through knowing
causes that must inevitably lead to it—but that which is
founded upon spiritual communications made to man from
the unseen spiritual world, and relating to matters which
are altogether outside of the power of human discernment.
If man would acquire worldly wisdom, he must desire it
and strive to obtain it. So with spiritual knowledge, if
he would gain the unfoldment of his spiritual nature, he
must live with a mind pure and in affinity with those
exalted beings who enjoy powers of observation beyond
that of mankind, and in all things follow that leading
precept of Jesus by living at one with the Father, studying
His will instead of his own, and living in harmony with
nature. John viii., Jesus said, "I have many things to
say, ... but He that sent me is true ; and I speak to
the world those things which I have heard of Him. . . . . .
He that sent me is with me ; the Father hath not left
me alone ; for I do always those things that please
Him." The great essential condition which must precede
SUPPLY is clearly shown throughout all the ramifications
of natural law to be WANT, or its equivalent in magnetic
attraction or affinity. Until people experience a want
of the divine spirit with knowledge and strength, and

are prepared to exert their efforts to attain it, they need not expect it. All the pre-received teachings of theology and tradition must be wiped from the mind, and that divine standard of right and wrong which we call conscience must be relieved from error, and thus adjusted to receive, as a new-born child, that divine light. Mark x., "Whosoever shall not receive the kingdom of God as a little child, he shall not enter therein." "The whole need no physician, but they that are sick." Those who are satisfied with tradition and theological teachings, and are not feeling a want of anything better, are not likely to obtain it. The strong man reliant in himself seeks no assistance, and the self-wise are above receiving wisdom. It is he who feels the utter insufficiency of worldly attainments, and desires in a child-like spirit the assistance of the Father, who is drawn to Him and taught of Him. The material or animal instincts must be negative, while relatively the spiritual promptings are positive, and the individual spiritual intelligence must be negative relatively to the Divine intelligence. Thus an at-one-ment is established. John vi., "I came not to do mine own will, but the will of Him that sent me."

"Man must be born again," as it were, and his conscientious convictions and divine promptings acted up to; and by thus keeping himself pure, and making the best use of powers at his disposal for the general good, he may receive additional gifts, for by revelation he may be taught of things beyond the power of observation of the material senses. "I thank thee," exclaimed Jesus at one time, "because thou hast hid these things from the wise and prudent, and hast revealed them unto babes." Before building the cost must be well estimated, however. If a man realise a want of something more substantial and satisfying to his higher nature than the pursuit of worldly gratifications, and he resolves to leave these off in order to cultivate his spiritual nature—if, after the purification of the earthly temple, he fails, like the character presented in Matt. xii. [who, having got rid of the unclean spirit, walked about seeking rest and finding none, and so went back to his own house to find it clean swept, garnished, and empty, and then longing for a return to self-gratification, allowed his animal cravings to regain their ascendancy over his spiritual nature, and thereupon sought the companionship of other spirits more wicked than himself], he will, like that character, find himself worse in the end. For, by the introduction thus to his "temple" of the inferior magnetism represented in the evil influences, in any after return to purity of purpose he will first have to overcome that law of nature which strengthens the attractive force between two things once brought together. Old affinities re-established must first be dissolved, and new affinities formed, before reform can take place. "I am come to send fire on the earth; and what will I, if it be already kindled?" —Luke xii. 49. Revelation is made through the law in nature of magnetic attraction; and all knowledge is conveyed to man through the fire of magnetic currents established at will, the which are mostly unseen by men, although they have been distinguished at times by some. [See other parts of this work referring to the laws governing mind.] The implanting of the high spiritual teachings of Jesus upon earth is the kindling of a fire, as spiritual growth is magnetic increase, through the higher magnetic influences attracted by the purer desires of more enlightened mind. "The kingdom of God," observed Jesus to the Pharisees (Luke xvii.), "is within you." "For as the lightning that lighteneth out of the one part under heaven, shineth unto the other part under heaven, so shall also the Son of man be in his day." So it is literally, for wherever two or three are met together in purity of desire to receive truth through him, he will come as a lightning-flash to the midst of them, "to bless them and to do them good." Convinced that an honest examination into revelation and the prevailing religious beliefs, and a sincere searching for the truths pertaining to the higher temporal and spiritual existence is not only warranted, but is actually necessary for the present elevation and the lasting happiness of mankind; and having indicated an unfailing basis on which to rear religious belief and find the best temporal and spiritual guidance, in ever open revelation checked by reason and the observed operations of law in material nature, it becomes necessary to investigate those laws which govern revelation and reason, and see what relation these bear to each other as well as to the laws which govern material nature. To this end it will not be necessary to go beyond the little we know of our own world, for it is shown that nature repeats itself in all its operations from the lower to the higher phases of existence. Our inquiries will be directed therefore chiefly to the consideration of the known character of those general laws which are observed to govern matter, the nature of the connection between mind and matter, and the intimacy between reason and revelation.

NATURAL RELIGION.

WHEN the reasoning man endeavours to estimate the connection between God and nature—mind and matter—he invariably begins with the endeavour to trace back from the effects the cause ; and thus, after he surveys the many evidences of unerring design in the orders of material nature around him, he looks upward, and after surveying there the further evidences of infinite wisdom displayed in the ordering of the resplendent "orbs of night," his mind dwells upon the unfathomable mysteries of time and space, and he stops to ask himself, What was " in the beginning " ? Thus commence the Scriptures, " In the beginning ;" and thus should every one, who is natural-minded enough to realise that he is here to learn of nature, ask himself, What was in the beginning?

In the beginning, according to Scripture, we are told, "the earth was without form, and void." The inference, of course, is, that it was not originally in the same condition that it is now in. No doubt there is a law of progression of existences applying to all things. Everything has its span of life in each existence. The flower may live one day, the forest tree a hundred years, and this earth itself many thousands ; and there is in all of these the state of infancy and of mature age in each existence. Thus, while we may expect but little knowledge in childhood, we wonder at the wisdom of a Shakespere in the prime of manhood. When, therefore, we accept the statement that our parent earth itself has taken thousands of years to reach its present condition, we must also acknowledge an expectation that it, too, in time will reach the span of its present existence and enter upon another. It cannot be annihilated, as it is a law of nature that matter may only change its form but cannot be annulled, and if there is any book from which we may glean truth, surely it is the book of nature—that book, the mere casual study of which convinces all races of the existence of an all-wise Creator and Ruler. Looking, then, at nature, we find things constantly changing form, living here and dying there, new combinations forming here and decaying there, while all are steadily and surely on the onward march of progress, extremes meeting in all things, hills being levelled with the valleys, and rough places being made smooth. The granite turns to moss, the moss to grass, and the grass, entering animal existence, reaches man. These stages show the rapid expansion of mind, as in each stage a greater degree of intelligence is acquired in the building up of a higher development of matter and spirit from the lower conditions. In all matter there is spirit, and in all spirit there is mind, although, of course, in the granite, for instance, we have a very elementary or low form of mind. With all the boasted self-wisdom of the age, and the knowledge acquired by investigating nature, there are many things very near and dear to all of us which neither the naturalist nor chemist have been able to detect nor analyse. The physician can tell you that if the functions of the heart be arrested by a wound or otherwise, that death will inevitably follow ; but he does not explain what the life principle in man is, nor the process by which that nerve current which gives action to the heart is provided for or sustained, and the chemist cannot tell what is the spirit of man. Such problems will some day be solved, for there is not anything hid but shall be revealed. At present we can only speculate as to what is the character of these subtle influences, and on entering upon this inquiry, it becomes necessary to premise, by pointing out that it is the custom of society not to receive any revelation of any newly-discovered force, or form of matter, without it be accepted by leading scientific minds; and these minds will not accept the existence of such things without the discoverers can demonstrate their existence to the satisfaction of their material senses. If it is said that soda can assume the form of a metal, the metal must be produced ; or if it is said electricity can be collected and utilised, it must be demonstrated in a way which the material senses can comprehend. The theorising of ancient philosophers does not fit the age, and he, who having once satisfied his own mind of the existence of a new force, often finds himself confronted with a greater task in being able to demonstrate its existence to the satisfaction of other minds, or reduce his discovery to purposes of general utility. There are in nature, however, certain laws and forces which are not visible to the eye, but the existence of which can nevertheless be demonstrated. The presence of certain gases, the law of specific gravity, electricity, and magnetism, for instance, may be demonstrated. Apart from such instances, there are others which show us that it is not wise to deny the existence of matters simply because the naked eye cannot detect them, or because we cannot feel, hear, smell, or taste them. Take a survey of the heavens, for instance, through a powerful telescope, or examine minutely through a microscope almost any material or liquid, and it will at once be apparent that there are more things in existence than our unaided material senses can detect. Again, there are other forces in nature the existence of which cannot be demonstrated by any process resembling those which prove to us the existence of such things as have been enumerated—such, for instance, as the action and force of the mind and will of man ; and yet, again, there are still other and more subtle forces which act upon the mind and will of man, the existence of which are self-evident to all men, a knowledge of them being inherited by all from nature. For this reason, when it is proposed to unfold the modes of action of some of those laws which appear to control the inner and unseen life of man, there is no proof tendered of their actuality further than that they are simply submitted to the inner consciousness of those whose minds can receive them. In matters of belief pertaining to the action of the laws of life, mind, spirit, there is no uniform standard of truth except in God or nature. Mathematical deductions, such as two and two make four, are not applied by theologians or scientific men to matters of religious belief. Each sect professes that its own peculiar doctrines alone represent truth, but as all are different, so all, it is held, cannot be correct. The fundamental religious principles in all these are, however, similar, for they are uniformly dictated by a natural conscience, and have ever been inculcated by all inspired teachers ; but errors, differences, and jealousies grow out of doctrinal points raised upon writings and deliverances which are held sacred by reason of coming through channels through which pure inspirational teachings have otherwise been received. It is worthy of note here, that Jesus invariably avoided doctrinal points, while he inculcated by his example and teachings sound moral and religious principles.

A mind may be expanded by special experiences to receive wider and fuller inspiration upon one subject, whilst, from a lack of similar expansion, it may not be able to receive inspiration of the same clear character upon another subject. Some minds may, however, by fervent continuous desire and strong holy purpose, attract, under favourable passive conditions, inspiration suited to the most expanded of minds ; whilst, on the other hand, from want of fervency and purity of purpose, or from the absence of conditions necessary for receiving pure inspiration from invisible intelligence from without, minds may be impressed by faulty spiritual agencies leading to error and mischief, and it is quite natural for the most inspired of teachers to inculcate error and mischief mixed with good and truth, for the best of human channels are not always clean, and that which passes through must be more or less polluted. In addition to this, more especially in Scripture held sacred, the interpretations of scholarship, by defects, or by too strict adherence to literal meanings, often change pure spiritual symbolical teachings into meaningless realities or obnoxious fiction, so that the base fabrications of the human mind are preached and taught and handed down from one generation to another under the guise of the divinely-inspired Word of God.

Max Müller, in speaking of languages, lays down as an incontrovertible general principle that "the original meaning of inscriptions written in a dead language, of which the tradition is once lost, can never be recovered." Hence all the labours of Grotefend, Burnouf, Lassin, and Rawlinson have been in vain, as he shows from their various readings of the same inscriptions and of their alterations of those renderings. "If there seems to be less change in the translation of the books of the Old Testament, or of Homer, it is due chiefly," he says, "to the absence of that critical exactness at which the decipherers of ancient inscriptions and the translators of the Veda and Zend-Avesta aim, in rendering each word that comes be-

fore them." If we compared the translation of the Septuagint with the authorised version of the Old Testament, we
should occasionally find discrepancies nearly as startling
as anything that can be found in the different translations of the cuneiform inscriptions or of the Veda and Zend-
Avesta. In Job, for instance, the Vulgate translates the
exhortation of Job's wife by, " Bless God and die ; " the
English version by, " Curse God and die ; " the Septuagint
by, " Say some words to the Lord and die." Though at the
time when the Seventy translated the Old Testament,
Hebrew could hardly be called a dead language, yet there
were then many of its words the original meaning of
which even the most learned Rabbi would have had great
difficulty in defining with real accuracy. " The meaning
of words changes imperceptibly and irresistibly." Even
when there is a printed literature like that of modern
Europe, four or five centuries work such a change that few
even of the most learned divines in England would find it
easy to read and to understand accurately a theological
treatise written in English four hundred years ago. The
same happened to a greater extent in ancient languages.
Nor was the sacred character attributed to certain writings
any safeguard ; on the contrary, greater violence is done by
successive interpreters to sacred writings than to any other
relics of ancient literature. Ideas grow and change, yet
each generation tries to find its own ideas reflected in the
sacred pages of their early prophets. And besides the
ordinary influences which blur and obscure the sharp features of old words, artificial influences are here at work dis-
torting the natural expression of words. "Parts of the Veda
or Zend-Avesta which do not bear on religious or philosophical doctrines are generally explained simply and naturally
even by the latest of native commentators," says Mr. Müller ;
"but so soon as any word or sentence can be turned to
support a doctrine, however modern, or a precept, however
irrational, the simplest phrases are tortured and mangled,
till at last they are made to yield their assent to ideas the
most foreign to the minds of the authors of the Veda and
Zend-Avesta." The Rev. R. G. S. Browne, in a small essay,
" Mosaic Cosmogony," says, as to the 1st chapter of Genesis, " What is the meaning or scope of the Hebrew verb in
our authorised version, rendered by ' created ' ? To Eng-

lish ears, by sound and long usage, it represents an *ex nihilo* creation, but in the teeth of all the rabbinical and cabalistic fancies of Jewish commentators, and with reverential deference to modern criticism on the Hebrew Bible, it is not so." Mr. Browne says the primary meaning of the word " barâ," from which " created " has been taken, is, " he cut, cut out, carved, planed down, polished." He refers to Mr. Lee, who characterises it as " a silly theory that ' barâ ' meant to create *ex nihilo.*" In Joshua xxii. 15 and 18, the same verb is used in the sense of " cutting down trees ; " in Psalm civ. 30, it is translated by " Thou renewest the face of the earth." In Arabia, too, " barâ " means properly, though not always, " to create out of pre-existing matter." This all shows that in the verb " barâ," as in the Sanskrit " toaksh " or " taksh," " there is no trace of the meaning assigned to it by later scholars, of a creation out of nothing." That idea, in its definiteness, was a modern idea, most likely called forth by the contact between Jews and Greeks at Alexandria. The Greek notion was, " matter was co-eternal with the Creator," while the Jews, to whom Jehovah was all in all, asserted for the first time deliberately, " that God had made all things out of nothing." And this became the received orthodox view of Jewish and Christian divines, although " barâ," so far from lending any support to that theory, would show that in those addressed by Moses it only called forth the simple conception of " fashioning "or " arranging." " The ancient history of the world," says Max Müller, " previous to 500 B.C., consists of mere lists of Egyptian, Babylonian, and Assyrian dynasties. The tablets of Karnak, the palaces of Nineveh, and the cylinders of Babylon tell nothing of the thoughts of man. There has been but one oasis in the vast desert of ancient history—the history of the Jews—another is the Veda. It is difficult to say whether the Veda is the oldest of books, or whether some portions of the Old Testament may not be traced back to the same or even an earlier date than the oldest hymns of the Veda ; but in the Aryan world the Rig-Veda is certainly the oldest book, and its preservation amounts almost to a marvel." At Alexandria, when the Old Testament was rendered into Greek, the Avesta was also translated into the same language, so that we have at Alexandria, in the third century B.C., a well-established historical contact between the believers in Genesis and the Avesta. The Zend MSS. of the Avesta are modern, so are the Hebrew MSS. of Genesis, which do not carry us beyond the tenth century after Christ. The text of the Avesta, however, can be checked by the Pehlevi translation made under the Sassanian dynasty (226–651 A.D.), just as the text of Genesis can be checked by the Septuagint translation made in the third century before Christ.

The language of India had so changed since the 600 B.C. (when the very verses, words, and syllables of the Veda had been counted) that about 300 B.C. learned commentaries were found necessary to explain the true purport and proper pronunciation of their hymns. " We may sup-" pose, remarks Mr. Müller, " that the earliest collection of the Vedic hymns was finished 1100 to 1200 years B.C., or 1500 B.C. for the original composition of the hymns of the fathers. Buddhism, whatever the date of its founder, became the State religion of India in the middle of the third century B.C., under Asoka, the Constantine of India. Previous to 1000 B.C. must be set apart for the free and natural growth of what was then *national* and *religious,* but not yet *sacred* and *sacrificial* poetry. Book revelation is not peculiar to Christianity. We do not find it in the literature of Greece and Rome, but the literature of India is saturated with it. Languages," continues Mr. Müller, " are now classed genealogically: the Aryan or Indo-European family, the Semitic family and the Turanian class. The English and all the Teutonic languages of the Continent—Celtic, Sclavonic, Greek, Latin, with its modern offshoots, as French and Italian—Persian and Sanskrit, are all varieties of one common type of speech. Sanskrit, the ancient language of the Veda, is no more distinct from the Greek of Homer, the Gothic of Ellfilas, or from the Anglo-Saxon of Alfred, than French is from Italian. The Semitic family comprises, as its most important members, the Hebrew of the Old Testament, the Arabic of the Koran, and the ancient languages on the monuments of Phœnicia and Carthage, of Babylon and Assyria; and these languages differ from the Aryan or Indo-European. The third group includes most of the remaining languages of Asia, and its principal members are the Tongusic, Mongolic, Turiet, Malay Islands, Tibet, and Southern India. Lastly, the Chinese stands by itself as monosyllabic—the only remnant of the earliest formation of human speech. The two religions of Aryan origin which survive, viz., Brahmanism and Buddhism, claim together a majority among the inhabitants of the globe. Out of the whole population of the world—

31·2 per cent. are Buddhists.
13·4   ,,   are Brahmanists.
——————
44·6

Of the remaining 56 per cent., 15·7 are Mohammedan, 8·7 are Heathen, 30·7 Christian, and only 3 Jews." In taking leave of the valuable testimony of Mr. Müller upon these matters, it may be observed that in the Chinese the same changes in the language have occurred. The writings of Confucius, for instance, although brief in themselves originally, have from time to time been enlarged upon and added to by others with a view to render the meanings of the characters used in the teachings of that great Chinese philosopher and reformer intelligible through the successive changes that have taken place in the forms of expression since his time (550 B.C.) To return, then, to the work in hand, it may be said that truth in the finite mind only represents, after all, so much of belief as the expansion of each individual mind can admit of, or receive, to understand; hence all are right in degree, while all are wrong in degree. Seen at different times, by each, the colours of the chameleon differ, and it is only the mind that knows the whole nature of the animal in respect to its change of colour that can be expected to have arrived at the truth. Some persons, too, are colour-blind without knowing it; and such have been known to swear that a certain thing was of a colour it appeared to them to be, while in reality it was proved by others to be of a different colour. It is the tendency to rely upon what has been told to us, or what we have seen, and the anxiety to proselytise or convince others into our own received opinions, which leads to so much error. "Woe unto you, scribes and Pharisees, hypocrites! for ye compass sea and land to make one proselyte, and when he is made, ye make him twofold more the child of hell than yourselves." A knowledge of the whole truth rests alone in the All-wise, and cannot be grasped by the finite mind, which must grow by actual personal experiences

acquired.   If mind is to expand with a knowledge of truth,
it must feel the need of spiritual enlightenment and yearn
for it.   " Seek, and ye shall find ; " " Knock, and it shall
be opened unto you."   It is by the universal law of attraction only that truth and purity are attained.   " No man
can come to me except the Father who hath sent me
draw him."   The mind ripens under its experiences, as
fruit, by a law of nature, ripens under the sun ; hence, in
season, it is " drawn " of the Father, and is in a condition
to receive the high spiritual teachings of a Jesus.   Jer. xxxi.,
" I will put my law in their inward parts, and write it in
their hearts. . . . They shall teach no more every man his
neighbour, and every man his brother, saying, Know the
Lord : for they shall all know me, from the least of them
unto the greatest."

The greatest calamity of the present age is the want of
spiritual concern—that spiritual sleep which comes out of
the universal practice amongst professing religionists of
delegating the care of their spiritual interests to paid
preachers.   " Carry neither purse, nor scrip, nor shoes,"
was a part of the injunction received by the disciples.
Whilst the parson is occupied in writing sermons and reading them as a matter of profession for a living, the church-
goers devote their whole time and energy to the acquisition
of worldly gain and distinctions, instead of each one working out his own salvation in an earnest desire, and yearning
for truth as it is in God and nature.   " Search the Scriptures, for in them ye think ye have eternal life, and they
are they which testify of me."   Error is the first condition
of " sin," as " evil " is but a perversion of good, and that is
a wise law which is constantly teaching all of us not to depend upon what we have been told, by making us constantly
suffer the necessarily consequent penalties of human misdirection, " inheriting the sins of the fathers," smarting
from the artificial customs of society, or from human and
erroneously conceived and executed laws, or from vitiated
tastes.

> " For *good* and *evil* must in our actions meet ;
> Wicked is not much worse than indiscreet."—*Donne.*

That human caprice makes great havoc of the affairs of nations is obvious from the manner in which wars are declared.

For instance, two representatives of nations meet to discuss a political matter; one of these thoughtlessly partakes of a heavy supper the previous night which disarranges his bile, and in bad temper he may use insulting language which the head of the nation addressed takes to heart, and which culminates in a declaration of war, in which thousands who had no part in the quarrel are led to sacrifice their lives, and other thousands of the equally innocent and poor who survive are taxed to pay the cost of. The laws of nature, unlike those of man, never alter, for they are designed by God in perfect wisdom. Convinced on this point, we are led inevitably to the conclusion that they are the very best standard of truth for man, and thus is set up the Religion of Nature. It is supposed that in man the spirit partakes of the same form as his material body, and that in life it permeates his whole system, as do the nerves. As the degree of utility and beauty in a house is represented by the materials of which it is constructed, the purposes for which it is used, its associations, and the mind which fashions it, so is the material body representative of the constitution it inherits, the food and air upon which it is built up, its associations, and the purposes for which it is used ; and so also it is only natural to conjecture that the immaterial spirit and mind of man are representative of what has been attracted to them. All beautiful spots in nature's scenery are not fashioned alike, and where nature has been most bare, we sometimes find that, by the skill of man, its very unevenness and ruggedness have been turned to things of extra beauty. So it is with the forms of mind in man, for sometimes in youth have been observed strong peculiarities causing the utmost uneasiness to parents, but which, having been placed to good account, afterwards produced to the world its greatest benefactors.

> " 'Tis with our judgments as our watches ; none
> Are just alike, yet each believes his own."—*Pope.*

" Even the best things," remarks Bishop Hall, " ill used, become evils, and contrarily, the worst things, used well, prove good. A good tongue used to deceit ; a good wit used to defend error ; a strong arm to murder ; authority to oppress ; a good profession to dissemble, are all evil. Even God's own Word is the sword of the Spirit, which, if it remove not our vices, pierces our souls. Contrariwise (as poisons are used to make

C

wholesome medicine) afflictions and sins, by a good use, prove so gainful as nothing more. Words are as they are taken, and things are as they are used. There are even cursed blessings."

It has often been pointed out by writers that man has a dual nature—namely, a temporal body and an eternal spiritual nature ; but it cannot be said that such a dual nature pertains alone to man, for, as already stated, all matter has spirit. The uniformity of the laws of nature become the more apparent the more they are examined into. The law of attraction and repulsion, for instance, by which are ruled the movements of those countless worlds which revolve within their respective orbits through limitless space with such marvellous precision, governs also all things on earth, and the very movements of man himself. With a material body and brain, representative of spirit and mind, man is governed in this existence, as he will no doubt be in the next, by the law of attraction and repulsion, having a certain orbit or sphere of existence within which he must move. This orbit is represented by his will-power and the functions of his body. He is endowed with a freedom of will and a freedom of action of a prescribed character in each existence ; and according as he exercises his will and efforts for good or evil, so does he, by a fixed law of nature, attract good or evil to himself, and by this law he builds up his own identity, which in itself constitutes a perfect and exact record of all his own actions in body and mind.

> "The secret that does make a flower a flower,
> So frames it that to bloom is to be sweet,
> And to receive to give.
> No soil so sterile, and no living lot
> So poor, but it hath somewhat still to spare
> In bounteous odours. Charitable they
> Who, by their having more or less, so have
> That less is more than need, and more is less
> Than the great heart's goodwill."—*Dobell.*

Every little bud that shows itself upon a plant represents the action of mind, a thought, an idea ; and that idea, from its inception—as well as that material form, the tiny bud, when first seen, and through which the idea is visibly expressed —contains all the elements of the peculiar form of material nature which that bud is destined to grow into. The plant having expressed thus, by a bud, its desire to grow in a certain direction, that mere mind-action grows into more extended mind-action, and these actions of the mind at every stage find expression in the growing visible form, which, from the first inception of the first idea of budding, necessarily grew in accordance with nature's established laws, for at every stage of its mind's exercise, nature brought to it WANTS to secure its maturity ; and thus, in the actions of the mind and in the progress of its visible expression, the material form drew or attracted, by its wants, sap from the mother plant, and light, air, and heat from the outer world to meet its requirements until it attained maturity; bore flowers and fruit, and in turn itself became the parent of another idea or bud. " Every tree," said Jesus, " is known by its fruit "—and this may well be applied to man, for, " as he sows, so shall he reap." As the inward mind in each bodily existence is exercised, so does the direction of that mind-exercise, the idea and desire, express itself upon the animal organisation or upon the organs of the brain and tastes. You cannot spoil the mind, but you can the material organisation through which it has to express itself. The most skilful musician cannot discourse harmonious sounds upon a shattered instrument, because the instrument is incapable of expressing mind-conceptions ; and you may not expect good fruit from a barked tree, because it cannot perform natural functions. The enslaving influences of drunkenness, smoking, &c., may thus be attributed to artificially-acquired wants, which people in their ignorance of the laws of nature unnecessarily and injuriously build up for themselves.

" Since, of desires, some are natural and necessary ; others natural but not necessary ; and others neither natural nor necessary, but the offspring of a wrong judgment : it must be the office of temperance to gratify the first class, as far as nature requires ; to restrain the second within the bounds of moderation ; and as to the third, resolutely to oppose, and, if possible, entirely repress them."—*History of Philosophy.*

The person who lends his mind to wrong a fellow-creature in order to acquire wealth, or fame, or self-gratification of any kind, by the very exercise of his mind in such a direction, strengthens within himself the desire to do other wrongs in a similar direction, so that he has no sooner accomplished one wrong than he WANTS the more strongly to do another larger wrong. The person who, on the other hand, is always on his guard against doing wrong to any one, and is ever exercising his ideas in a wish to do good to others, thus strengthens the higher organisation of his brain, keeps the lamp of his inward consciousness well trimmed, and improves apace both the material instrument and the eternal mind by thus laying up for himself " treasure in heaven." Shaftesbury remarks—

"Never did any soul do good, but it came readier to do the same again, with more enjoyment. Never was love or gratitude or bounty practised, but with increasing joy, which made the practiser still more in love with the fair act."

Seneca said, "He that does good to another does also good to himself, not only in the consequences, but in the act itself; " while Milton gives out that, "Good the more communicated, more abundant grows." The actions of thoughts record themselves as if upon a living tree for good or for evil ; and every evil thought or desire is like a bad branch put forth, for it not only deforms the tree, but it robs the good branches of the nutriment which they should receive through the parent stem. "It is from the remembrance of joys we have lost," remarks Mackenzie, "that the arrows of affliction are pointed." At death, the mind awakens with overpowering remorse and concern upon seeing, through its enlarged powers of comprehension, so clearly all those bad branches it had put forth, and the many evil consequences to which they have led, because that they were allowed to grow instead of being pruned off in time to allow of the better growth of the tree in its season of material being in the earth-life. It feels joy, however, at distinguishing, with equal clearness, those parts of natural growth in the tree, representing the good of a lifetime ; and it then takes courage to endeavour to amend, by cultivating those good parts. But this is done amidst all the difficulties which are presented by those evil deformities into which the tree had been suffered to grow ; for, although at death, the tree is unearthed, as it were, and the material form decays, yet the spirit-form envelops the eternal mind, and the evil influences of the deformed growth, with their bad consequences, have to be outgrown and overcome with sincere contrition and earnest good purpose. " Aspiration after the holy," says a distinguished writer, " is the only aspiration in which the human soul can be assured that it will never meet with disappointment." Another authority remarks : " What we truly and earnestly aspire to be, that in some sense we are. The mere aspiration, by changing the frame of the mind, for the moment realises itself." The exercise of the will-power or desire, as the law of want and supply, or attraction and repulsion, is found not only to be the law under which man may become spiritually strong in mind for good or evil, but it is the law under which he acquires genius in the arts and other walks of life. Ruskin has stated that—

" The clinging to and striving after first principles of beauty is ever the characteristic of the poet ; whether he speak a truth to the world through a pen, the perfect statue, or the lofty musical strain, he is still the sharer in the same high nature. Next to blind Milton describing Paradise, deaf Beethoven bending over his piano composing symphonies and oratorios —strains which he himself could never hope to hear—is one of the finest things we know. The sense of beauty was upon them, and they fain must speak. Arts may be learned by application ; proportions and attitudes may be studied and repeated ; mathematical principles may be comprehended and adopted ; but there has not yet been hewn from marble a second Apollo, and no measuring by compasses will ever give the secret of its power. The ideal dwelt in the sculptor's mind, and his hands fashioned a statue which yet teaches it to the world. It is an incarnation of fancy, and is a sort of petrified poetry, or concrete rhetoric."

Baldwin Brown, on the same subject, remarks—

" Very sacred is the vocation of the artist, who has to do directly with the works of God, and interpret the teaching of creation to mankind. All honour to the man who treats it sacredly ; studies, as in God's presence, the thoughts of God which are expressed to him ; and makes all things according to the pattern which He is ever ready to show to earnest and reverent genius on the mount."

" Our minds are so constructed "—remarks Sir Benjamin Brodie—" that we can keep the attention fixed on a particular object until we have, as it were, looked all around it ; and the mind that possesses this faculty in the highest degree of perfection will take cognisance of relations of which another mind has no perception. It is this, much more than any difference in the abstract power of reasoning, which constitutes the vast difference between the minds of different individuals. This is the history alike of the poetic genius, and of the genius of discovery in science. 'I keep the subject,' said Sir Isaac Newton, 'constantly before me, and wait until the dawnings open by little and little into a full light.' It was thus that after long meditation he was led to the invention of fluxions, and to the anticipation of the modern discovery of the combustibility of the diamond. It was thus that Harvey discovered the circulation of the blood; and that those views were suggested by Davy which laid the foundation of that grand series of experimental researches which terminated in the decomposition of the earths and alkalis."

" We should accustom ourselves "—recommends Dr Ferrier— " to make attention entirely the instrument of volition. Let the will be determined by the conclusions of reason—by deliberate conclusions—and then let attention be wielded by both. Think what is self-government ; what is fittest to be done ought to be now done, and let will be subordinate to reason, and attention to will. In this way you will be always disengaged for present duty. Pleasures, amusements, inferior objects, will be easily sacrificed to the most important. You may have likings to inferior or trifling occupations ; but if, to use the strong language of Scripture, you *crucify* these, oppose them, carry your intention beyond them, their power to molest and mislead you will decline."

It is said of a celebrated author that, when asked whether he believed in a future state of eternal punishment, he remarked that if there was such a destiny for him, he thought he would be allowed the privilege, before being condemned, of arguing the point of the justice of such a punishment. The laws of God are happily unlike those of man ; for mind being self-registering and self-purifying by the laws governing its action, there will be no necessity for judge or jury in the after-state ; nor can there arise, by any possibility, any error of judgment as to our proper destiny. There are many minds that cannot recognise that all that is, is right, and these are they who require to set up strange gods to themselves—gods presenting all the defects of their own darkened minds. They call them all-wise, all-power-ful, ever-present, all-loving ; yet they also, by some stretches of imagination, attribute to them error, regret, hatred, jealousy, absence, anger, &c. As man counts time, there can be no doubt that mind takes a long time to become sufficiently developed for that state of existence in which it no longer requires a material body. In each of the numerous gradatory forms through which it passes, from the time it leaves the granite, it picks up such additional experiences as each form admits of. Each creature which it enters is just that which yields of its kind, to it, that particular instinct which it wants most. The spirit-state being the connecting link in nature which bridges over all distinctions of species, is not seen, and therefore not understood to man. There are, however, some very close resemblances between the received orders of nature : the functions of the *Dionæa muscipula* or Venus' flytrap and sensitive plants, are found, for instance, to resemble very closely those of animals, while in the transition from the grub to the butterfly the spirit-link between two different material forms may be easily traced. And this reminds us of the lines on the butterfly by Rogers—

> "Child of the sun ! pursue thy rapturous flight,
> Mingling with her thou lov'st in fields of light,
> And where the flowers of paradise unfold,
> Quaff fragrant nectar from their cups of gold :
> There shall thy wings, rich as an evening sky,
> Expand and shut with silent ecstasy :
> Yet wert thou once a worm—a thing that crept
> On the bare earth, then wrought a tomb and slept.
> And such is man !—soon from his cell of clay
> To burst a seraph in the blaze of day."

The law of re-incarnation is not readily received by those who only give a passing effort of mind to its consideration. If the Spirit of God is in all things, and there is mind in all according to degree, from the crumb of granite to the angel, it is only natural to infer that at each progressive state of existence the intelligence should reside in a more beautiful tenement. John once exclaimed, " I say unto you, God is able of these stones to raise up children to Abraham." Few minds are open to understand the existence of such a law of nature up to the time of the spirit reaching man ; at this stage, however, from numerous instances that might be quoted, it is commonly acknowledged, but still there is much confusion of ideas on the subject. An exploded one, because of its violation of the principle of progression observed in nature, is : that the spirits of the bad may be re-incarnated in the lower animals. The theological idea of Christ's re-incarnation is : that " He might draw up into his own experience all the woes and temptations of humanity." Some savage races, such as the natives of Australia hold it possible for " black man die, jump up white man." There are many Biblical passages which might be quoted in support of re-incarnation. Jesus, for instance, when questioned as to how it was that the prophecy respecting the coming again of Elias before him had not been fulfilled, is represented in Matthew to have said, " If ye will receive it " Elias has already come as John the Baptist. " He that hath ears to hear, let him hear." John himself denied that he was Elias, when asked, for he had no recollection of pre-existence. The laws governing memory, or the recollections of a single lifetime even, are as yet very little understood. As an instance of this, people, when brought by accident very close to death, have been known to experience a vivid mind-flash of the whole doings of a lifetime within the space of about two· or three seconds of time—including recollections of things, too, which had long been forgotten. The greatest doubt amongst those who have considered the subject exists upon the point as to whether the spirit of man after death, and a certain period of mental purification and repose in the spirit world, and a pruning off or burning out of certain recollections, not necessary to perfection of the mind, may not be attracted to and re-incarnated in another human body in a different sphere of life, where experiences of a character, not already acquired, may be obtained. This will make a queen of a washerwoman and a king of a beggar, and, so to speak, " every dog will have his day."

Seneca said that—

" The origin of all mankind was the same ; it is only a clear and a good conscience that makes a man noble, for that is derived from heaven itself. It was the saying of a great man, that if we could trace our descents, we should find all slaves to come from princes, and all princes from slaves ; and fortune has turned all things topsy-turvy in a long series of revolutions ; beside, for a man to spend his life in pursuit of a title that serves only when he dies to furnish an epitaph, is below a wise man's business."

To trace the operations of such a law in nature as that of incarnation so as to be satisfied of its actuality, is to be possessed of internal evidence of the most powerful character of the immeasurable force and intrinsic worth of the leading precept of Jesus, viz., the brotherhood of mankind, and the expediency of its at-one-ment. While Jesus at an early age was teaching the people, his parents, who had missed him, having discovered his whereabouts, he was told that "they were without, desiring to speak to him," when, stretching forth his hands towards his disciples, in the words in Matt. xii. : Behold my mother and my brethren ; for whosoever shall do the will of my Father which is in heaven, the same is my brother, and sister, and mother," he proclaimed one of the most majestic truths in God's most magnificent ordering of nature. These words are repeated in Matt. xxiii. : "Call no man your father upon the earth, for one is your Father, which is in heaven." If people could only realise that one man was as much a creature of God as another, there might be more brotherly love in the world ; and if they could also realise their close connection to their beasts of burthen, such as their horses and their oxen, they might show more kindness to these dumb relations of theirs. The rich man who fared sumptuously every day, after death was reminded, "Thou in thy lifetime receivedst thy good things, and likewise Lazarus evil things ; but now he is comforted and thou art tormented." Certain worldly experiences being necessary to educate the mind for a more progressed existence out of a material body, the mind in the dying infant, if not already developed, will not escape that education, but must complete it in other bodies. Rachel weeping for her children because they were not, was told her work would be rewarded, for that they should come again from the land of the enemy, and there would be hope in her end, and that her children would come again to their own border. It would appear from Scriptural testimony that the minds of men do reside in more than one body, or are re-incarnated. There is room to believe also, not only that minds are re-incarnated in infancy, but that, by a law of absorption, from affinity or attraction, they may also be re-incarnated in individuals during manhood. The physical constitution of the material body of every person in life is, indeed, a proof in itself of the correctness of the theory of re-incarnation, for it has been received generally that every particle, including bone

in man, is renewed every seven years, while the softer parts
are renewed much more frequently; so that in life our
souls or invisible intelligence must necessarily inhabit completely renewed, or, in fact, other bodies, every seven years.
According to Luke, when the angel Gabriel appeared to
Zacharias and foretold that Elisabeth should bear a son
who should be called John (the Baptist), he said, " He shall
go before him (*i.e.*, Jesus), in the spirit and power of Elias."
Again, Jesus is represented to have said to his disciples,
" There be some standing here who shall not taste of death
till they see the Son of Man coming in his kingdom;"
which appears to mean, that some of them would continue
their experiences on the earth by being re-incarnated in
other bodies, or otherwise, until such time as his second
coming. " I pray not that thou shouldest take them out of
the world " (John xvii. 15). Theologians believe that
Jesus existed before the world. " Glorify me . . . with
the glory which I had with thee before the world was "
(John xvii. 5). " For thou lovedst me before the foundation of the world " (ver. 24). Although Jesus was then
good and happy, yet he underwent the pains and trials of
earth-life, and his coming again, even the " second coming "
upon this earth, is yet looked for by Christians. The earth
appears to have been given to earth-spirits to cultivate and
improve as the figurative Eden was given to Adam; and it
is doubtful whether any spirit belonging to it can get away
from it entirely until it is so spiritualised and cultivated as
to become a veritable " heaven," or a happy and fit abode
for the godly. Jesus, it is held, was an older spirit from a
more advanced planet, and in support of this he is represented to have said, " Ye are from beneath; I am from
above : ye are of this world; I am not of this world "
(John viii.) Again, John the Baptist is represented to
have used similar language as to Jesus, for in John iii.,
when he was told that Jesus was baptizing, he said, " A
man can receive nothing, except it be given him from
heaven . . . I am not the Christ . . . but I am sent before
him . . . he that cometh from above is above all : he that
is of the earth is earthly, and speaketh of the earth."
Under a high law of sympathy, in the will of the Father,
he desired to sow the seed of advanced truth in the growing minds of earth-spirits, and so he willed his incarnation

in earth-life, and thus attracted to and incarnated in it, he became " the way, the truth, and the life " to us who are drawn to the Father through the divine light made manifest to our minds through the exalting teachings of Christ. " For I came down from heaven not to do mine own will, but the will of Him that sent me ". (John vi.). Hence it is indicated as the first duty of all to make the most of their earth-lives in improving the condition of all people. And the intimate connection and great interest which earth minds (in or out of the body) should take in the affairs of this life, would appear to be indicated by the dual nature of man, for he is not only endowed with material brain, and body with animal life, but he has an invisible presence in mind (or soul) with its spiritual body, which is, as it were, the guardian angel-part of his materialised being during his earth life. Although to Christians, Christ is obviously " the way, the truth, and the life," to us by reason of his high pre-existent state, and the enlightenment which, through it, he was enabled to shed upon our minds from the Father, it is not clear that he has been the only exalted mind from more advanced worlds that has been attracted, by like godly sympathy, and incarnated in earth bodies. There have been other great minds engaged in illuminating this world in parts where, as a great spiritual leader, Jesus has not yet been generally recognised. In fact, we can form little or no conception of what we really owe to minds from more advanced planets than our own in God's universe. And, were we to dwell upon this phase, a certain direction of thought might lead us to ask whether it is not reasonable to suppose that the progenitors of man and species, with their sexes, suited to the earlier capabilities of a new world, might not have been transplanted on various parts of this earth from other planets ; for, although there are evidences that mind is progressive, coming up from the mineral or lower forms, yet it is questionable whether the time which would be occupied in making a man from the earth, would not far exceed the time which has elapsed since our world was inhabitable and the time back to which man can be traced. Why may we not suppose that the parent stock of races on our earth was conveyed here by some such law in nature as that of the magnetic sphere, by means of which weighty articles and even persons have been known in our own day to be enveloped and conveyed by unseen spiritual intelligence even through the walls of closed rooms? What is to prevent even the peopling of our own Moon in the same manner, so soon as it is known to be in a suitable condition to sustain life? Its distance is only equal to that of a few voyages to Australia! "The Spirit of God caught away Philip, that the eunuch saw him no more: and he went on his way rejoicing. But Philip was found at Azotus, and passing through he preached in all the cities" (Acts viii.). There does not appear to be anything unnatural or God-dishonouring in supposing that the more exalted spiritual dwellers of older worlds may have been commissioned, through impression, in obedience to divine will, to implant man and species upon this earth when it became ready to receive them.

"Let not your charity," says Henry Martyn, "stop with home, family, connections, neighbours, but look abroad. Look at the universal church, and, forgetting its divisions, be a catholic Christian. Look at your country, and be a patriot; look at the nations of the earth, and be a philanthropist."

Increase and multiply is one of the chief commissions given to all forms of life, or, wherefore are there sexes and germs through all nature?

"The happiness of mankind," remarks Coleridge, "is the *end* of virtue, and truth is the knowledge of the *means;* which he will never seriously attempt to discover who has not habitually interested himself *in the welfare of others.* The searcher after truth must love and be beloved; for general benevolence is begotten and rendered permanent by social and domestic affections. Paternal and filial duties discipline the heart, and prepare it for the love of all mankind."

To the figurative Adam was given Eve and Eden, and man now cultivates the soil for his sustenance, and feels conscious of having fulfilled a part of his mission when he has brought up good, healthy children.

Mary Howitt expresses a truly womanly and noble heart, when she says, "My soul blesses the great Father every day, that He has gladdened the earth with little children."

To suppose that higher beings have higher duties, such as implanting forms of life upon new worlds, and cultivating the higher forms of mind, is therefore only natural by inference. To return, however, to the laws governing the mind of man in the earth-life, when mind has progressed sufficiently to inhabit the form of man, it is only natural it should primarily, in this habitation, be found self-indulgent and selfish in all material matters, with very few of those rare and exalted qualities which distinguish the more spiritualised man. Indeed, so long as mind has not completed the probationary education for the immaterial existence, and requires for that purpose to inhabit the body of man, it is obviously essential for the proper protection and nourishment of that body that it should be endowed with the usual instincts of the material nature. If hunger and thirst were not felt, proper nourishment would be neglected ; if pain were not experienced, the care and protection of the body would be neglected ; if there were not sensual proclivities, there would be no increase ; and if there were no inherent love of offspring, the young would be neglected, and so on. The body is an essential residence for mind, as well as being an educator of it, in a certain stage of its existence and education on this planet, just as the body itself requires covering and a place of abode, which must be built, and kept in order and repair. Some men know no restraint to their animal indulgences, except in those pains which, in self-protection, their material forms impose, and so they become virtuous because they cannot indulge. As Paul puts it, " That was not first which is spiritual, but that which is natural, and afterwards that which is spiritual." Although, in the early man, his almost entire care is for his material wants, as the mind expands and ripens for another and higher state of existence, it recognises that, as far as self and the transitory material indulgences are concerned," all is vanity and vexation of spirit," and that it profits a man nothing if in gaining the whole world he lose his own soul.

Milton says—

" He that can apprehend and consider vice with all her baits and seeming pleasures, and yet abstain, and yet distinguish, and yet prefer that which is truly better, he is the true wayfaring Christian. I cannot praise a fugitive and cloistered virtue unexercised, and unbreathed, that never sallies out and sees her adversary, but slinks out of the race when that immortal garland is to be run for, not without dust and heat."

Matthew Henry holds that—

"It is more to the honour of a Christian soldier by faith to overcome the world, than by a monastical vow to retreat from it."

Göethe is under the impression that—

"Talents are nurtured best in solitude,
But character on life's tempestuous sea."

The ripening mind, whilst feeling the obligation of keeping its earthly temple clean and healthy, gives its chief care then to its spiritual welfare in loving and doing good to others, and being guided by the inner voice of conscience, making all the concerns of the material nature subservient to it. "What!" exclaimed St. Paul, "know ye not that your body is the temple of the Holy Ghost which is in you?" Its motto ever is, "God is my guide;" "Not my will, but thine be done."

"The consciousness of doing that which we are reasonably persuaded we ought to do," remarks Bishop Mant, "is always a gratifying sensation to the considerate mind: it is a sensation by God's will inherent in our nature; and is, as it were, the voice of God Himself, intimating His approval of our conduct, and by His commendation encouraging us to proceed."

In considering the action of those subtle forces outside of man, yet which act upon and control him, such, for instance, as inspiration or impression, it becomes necessary, first, to inquire what is life, and how is it sustained. The bodily organs being in health, with proper food, respiration, and circulation, life is supposed to continue its ordinary span; yet blood does not circulate of itself. The sustaining life-principle must be looked for, primarily, in the organic process which sustains the nerve-current, and in the presence of the spiritual co-operative forces. The spirit is not self-sustaining, neither is the body self-sustaining, but while the spirit is in the body it is sustained through it, and the body could not exist without it, so that they are dependent, in the material life, upon each other to a certain extent. As the life of the body is dependent upon the presence of spirit, so is the blood circulation dependent upon the action of the nerve-current, and in like manner the blood circulation and nerve-current mutually exist through each other, and both are thus sustained by the food and air taken into the body. At this stage, we have man presented to us having body and brain with their immaterial essence of spirit and intelligence residing with, subsisting upon, and mutually supporting each other. The brain is adapted to control and direct, at the will of the material sympathies and the invisible spiritual intelligence, the exercise of the sensuous nature and the functions and motions of the body, as well as to receive and profit by those aspirations of the nobler, higher, and spiritual being ; while the body, in return for the guiding intelligence it receives through the brain, and for its nerve-power, supplies through the blood circulation the material from which that nerve-force is generated, as well as the apparatus for locomotion wherewith the mind may pick up its experiences. It is now necessary to point out the distinctive relation which electricity and magnetism bear to each other, and what part these occupy in relation to life itself and those subtle forces by which man is controlled. Electricity, then, is simply the outcome of magnetism—*i.e.*, it is generated by the coming into contact of particles or elements having a magnetic affinity for each other. Observe, for instance, in the coming storm, those dark clouds moving from opposite directions towards each other. The commonplace observer will say they are drifted by opposite currents of wind ; whereas, being heavily surcharged with particles or elements in magnetic affinity with each other, they are simply attracted or drawn to each other ; and the immediate effect of contact is the generation of electricity ; and the result, a new combination commonly called "thunderbolt." The force which enables the telegraph operator to send messages great distances so quickly, is obtained in a similar manner. Copper and zinc being submerged in acid, the elements of which these metals are composed are rapidly liberated, and being in magnetic affinity with each other, find a rapid channel in the liquid for rushing together, thus generating the electricity required. If this definition be established, it should facilitate invention, so as to overcome those difficulties which have hitherto been experienced in all attempts to apply electric force to labour-saving machinery. The bulk and cost of apparatus, in proportion to the power obtained, together with the difficulty of controlling electric power, have been the great hindrances hitherto. Premis-

ing the definition to be correct, inventors will have a track
cleared for them : first, to discover which elements contain
most magnetic affinity, generating the most electricity most
rapidly and inexpensively, and the most compact apparatus ;
and having done this, the controlling or power-governing
difficulty may be overcome by partially or wholly regulating
it according to the rate of feeding the apparatus.   The
question before us in this place, however, is to identify the
life-principle of man with magnetism and electricity.   To
this end it is contended that the air and food taken into
the human system contain elements in magnetic affinity
with each other ; that these in the process of blood-making
or circulation (perhaps between the spleen, liver, and brain)
are liberated, generating a force identical with electricity,
and that this force or nerve-current is utilised for respiration, circulation, &c., and the nerve or muscular movements or sensations by the action of the will-power in the
brain and otherwise.   This partially explains that beautiful
reciprocal action between the blood-circulation and nerve-
current and muscular force, which works the heart, for the
heart cannot move without the nerve-current, and the nerve-
current cannot exist without the blood-circulation.   The
investigation of this theory by anatomists should lead to
important results, by indicating the best course of medical
treatment to pursue in cases where depression and a want
of activity in the circulation is observed.   Physical exertion, or an expenditure of nerve-power, generally induces
vigorous breathing, and appetite and fatigue induces rest.
Heavy eating, where there is strong digestive power, often
induces sleep where there is not sufficient exercise to work
off the superabundant nerve-power generated, and thus
man is often protected from his appetite.   On the other
hand, where little exercise is taken, and the digestive
powers are unequal to the work before them, sleeplessness
inducing mental exertion, and consequently an expenditure of nerve-force follows, and then, in turn, the digestive powers are relieved by a greater demand being made
upon them.   Professor Liebig, in speaking on the nerves,
says—

    " They accomplish the voluntary and involuntary motions of
the body ; they are the conductors of vital force ; they propagate motion, and behave towards other causes of motion, which

in their manifestations are analogous to the vital force, in a precisely analogous manner. They permit the current to traverse them, and present, as conductors of electricity, all the phenomena which they exhibit as conductors of vital force."

An eminent medical man says—

" The nervous system consists of two portions, one presiding over sensation and voluntary motion, hence called the sentient and the motive portions ; the other destitute of sensation, but presiding over the organic processes, hence called the organic portion. If the communication between the organic organ and the organic nerve be interrupted, the function of the organ, whatever it be, is arrested. Without its organic nerves the stomach cannot secrete gastric juice ; the consequence is, that the aliment is undigested. Without its organic nerves, the liver cannot secrete bile ; the consequence is that the nutritive part of the aliment is incapable of being separated from its excrementitious portion. The organic organ receives from its organic nerve an influence without which it cannot perform its function, but the nerve belonging to this class neither feels nor communicates feeling, and hence it imparts no consciousness of the operation of any process dependent on it."

" Each sentient nerve before it goes out to the animal organs to which it is destined to communicate sensation, sends off two branches to the organic or the non-sentient. Those sentient nerves mix and mingle with the insensible nerves, accompanying them in their course to the organic organs, and ramify with them throughout their substance. It is manifest, then, that sentient nerves, that nerves not necessary to the organic processes, having, as far as is known, nothing whatever to do with those processes, enter as constituent parts into the composition of the organic nerves. What is the result ? That organic organs are rendered sentient ; that organic processes, in their own nature insensible, become capable of affecting consciousness."

Another authority says—

" All diseases are caused by impressions made on the nervous centres, or their nerves, by which the nervous influence (whatever it be) is exhausted or diminished ; that the blood-vessels in health are in a state of semi-contraction, by virtue of this nervous influence. In disease, the nerves are relaxed and weakened, thus the diameter of the blood-vessels is enlarged, admitting a larger current of blood, whose motion becomes slower, and this is simple congestion when in the veins ; when in the arteries, it is accompanied by degeneration of the arterial coats, and is then called inflammation. This degeneration does not take place in the veins, because there is no oxidised blood there."

D

Another high medical authority says—

"A brain (and, consequently, every nervous centre) can no more give out efficient manifestations of force without a sufficient blood-supply than an army could fight or manœuvre effectively with a defective or missing commissariat, or an engine work up to its full power without a liberal supply of coal and water."

And a learned professor says—

"The results of experiments which he had himself made had shown the utmost importance of a proper arterial blood-supply to the brain. He had found from experiments on numerous animals that when, owing to the operations necessary to expose the brain, the blood-supply was lowered to a very great extent, the brain immediately ceased to give any action. When a brain was acting properly, with a circulation flowing through it freely, it reacted to a slight stimulus of electricity ; but when the heart was very weak, and the animal had lost a great deal of blood, he might apply any stimulus, however powerful, to the brain, and it would not react. Moreover, he had seen animals which had lost a great quantity of blood in that way fall asleep, and any stimulation would entirely fail to awaken them."

Having endeavoured to indicate what relation magnetism and electricity bear to the life principle, and how life is sustained, it now becomes necessary to consider the nature of those laws by which the brain and mind of man is acted upon from without. As already stated, the brain, at the will of the material sympathies and the invisible spiritual intelligence, is adapted to control and direct the exercise of the sensuous nature and the functions and motions of the body, as well as to receive and profit by those aspirations of the nobler spiritual being, by the instrumentality of the nerve-current, or magnetism and electricity. Under certain electro-biological conditions, where, by passes and otherwise, the animal magnetic and electric currents are connected between two persons, one yielding a passive assent and submitting to the control of the other person, he can be made to believe, think, or do anything almost which the one controlling wills. If the controller tells him the house is on fire, for instance, although such is not really the case, he believes it and acts accordingly. Here, then, is cited a case where it is obvious that the material brain of one man in the body may, without reference to his own individual invisible intelligence or mind, control and exercise his whole nature under the will and mind intelligence of another man in the body. It is obvious, therefore, first, that the mind or directing intelligence is spiritual or immaterial; second, that the functions of the body and brain are directed by it; third, that the directing mind or intelligence at will may retire, and allow the control of the material organism to another intelligence; and fourth, that other mind or intelligence may exercise control by means of the establishment of a current of magnetism or electricity. Such should be the nature of the influence at the " laying on of hands " at ordination, provided the wills of those officiating have first been made subservient to the will of the Father, and their minds rest on pure, fervent, and holy purposes, otherwise the ceremony is worse than a mockery.

At this stage we have unfolded to us that inestimable blessing in that beautiful law under which inspiration or impression is received; that law under which the man Adam is so beautifully and figuratively exhibited to us in Eden communing with God. The mind or directing intelligence of man is not lost at death, but exists after that in a spiritual body; and by the law of attraction, affinity, or sympathy, it is drawn to us, so that, by a passive assent under favourable circumstances, it may control us as positively and fully while it is out of the material body as it might have done under electro-biological conditions while in the body. The mind or directing intelligence of man is an emanation from the Father, and those who, by continuous holy aspiration, wish to make their material desires subservient to the will of God, draw, by natural law, inspirational influences suited to their development or capacity to receive, and thus live, as did our great Exemplar, AT ONE with the Father and nature. Minds being governed by attraction or affinity, there is as much difficulty to bring those that may be at variance together, as there is to mix oil with water. Hence, the mind which purposes evil, or is all absorbed with the desire of worldly gain, may not expect pure outside influences, but may attract to it the influence of spirits of deceased persons in sympathy with it, or whose minds while on earth were similarly employed, and whose desires have not much altered; and this accounts for many murders done on sudden impulse by those who had previously nursed evil and wicked thoughts against their victims, without any premeditated intention or desire, however, to take away life. The operation of such a law should persuade us of the evil effects of capital punishment, as the mere taking away of life does not reform the mind, nor stay its evil influence upon society. Instruction, cleanliness, with inducements to reform, and with continuous appropriate occupation, would do more for criminals. It would be better, even, to supply them with seed and an isolated country to cultivate.

A wider knowledge of those unseen influences controlling the thoughts and actions of criminals and the insane, will enable man to deal more charitably and effectively with them. Conditions of marriage, which the law might be altered to take cognisance of, may be held responsible for the causation of a large proportion of these ; while their remedy or alleviation will be more effectual if efforts are directed to restoring harmony or equilibrium between the positive and negative nerve forces, as insanity resides chiefly in the unequal distribution of the animating forces, in the imponderables and not in the solids, or in the connection between the invisible controlling influence and the material organism to be controlled, through receptive defects in the material organism—generally of hereditary origin, but sometimes through their own abuse of natural laws. The singular influence which may be exerted over an insane man by an experienced wardsman by a simple firm glance from the eyes, may, from this reason, be accounted for. The eye can emit magnetism, and by means of the eyes alone a magnetic current may be established, by which one mind may control the organism of another person, as in electro-biology, referred to elsewhere. In the insane man, the magnetic current from the eyes of the wardsman acts upon the connection between the invisible controlling influence and the material organism, and restores the equilibrium, by imparting to the latter a participation in the more healthy material organism of the wardsman. With persons detected in the perpetration of a wrong action, a single glance will often stir up an inward conviction, not till then experienced through a growing disuse of conscience. These matters require greater attention, however, than can be given to them in this place, as the object is more to deal with the operation of healthy minds. To this end, it may be remarked that, when the mind is developed or spiritualised, and feels a yearning for the pure and holy above the material gratifications, when the earthly " self " has been crucified, and the man is " born again," then will be realised the meaning of the following and many other scriptural passages :—" I will put my law in their inward parts. They shall teach no more every man his neighbour, and every man his brother, saying, Know the Lord, for they shall all know me. . . . I shall remember their sin no more. . . . For it sufficeth that in times past we have walked in the lusts of the flesh. . . . They shall be taught of God," &c.

> " Though affliction, at the first, doth vex
> Most virtuous natures, from the sense that 'tis
> Unjustly laid ; yet, when the amazement which
> That new pain brings is worn away, they then
> Embrace oppression straight, with such
> Obedient cheerfulness, as if it came
> From heaven, not man."—*Davenant.*

Baldwin Brown speaks of discipline thus—

" To a certain extent, we can all see that discipline is good for us. What man of business repents him of the time he spent in what appeared to be the sharp discipline of school ? Tell me which of you came through childish and youthful follies without sharp lessons ? Who has not been bitterly mortified by the wounding of his self-importance, or heartily laughed at for what he thought very wise and grand ? Looking back upon all those sharp lessons, you would rather they had been stronger, so as to have killed your weaknesses at their very root. We see so far, then, that good comes out of discipline ; and hereby you consent to the wisdom of the discipline of God."

What is intended to be conveyed, or what is the most profitable meaning to be taken from the words, " I shall remember their sin no more " ? Relieved from mystery, and applying it to our own times and requirements, we should say that he who exercises his thoughts in ignorance or from want of experience in such a way as to weaken the capacity for good of his brain organism commits " sin ;" he who acts towards mankind in such a way as to propagate error or to injure them otherwise, commits " sin." He who, by careful watching, weeds out, at their earliest inception, all thoughts of evil intent or of a debasing nature injurious to his own brain organism or to that of others, "blots out his sins" or defects, by improving his mind capacity; and he who devotes his mind and energies to the study of God's natural laws, and to the propagation of that knowledge in purity to others, or who devotes his best energies to enterprises which confer good on mankind, lays up for himself "treasure in heaven;" for, what happiness can surpass that which will be realised by that mind which, when relieved from the cloudy obscurities of the material existence, awakens in the spiritual world, and beholds with clearness and satisfaction the beautiful outgrowth of its efforts for good while in the earth-life? Not anything is left to chance in nature. Worlds, revolving in space, travel millions of miles, completing their annual orbits to a fraction of a second. The very hairs of our heads, so to speak, are numbered. The birds of the air, the fish of the sea, the wild beasts of the woods, ay, and the most minute insects which the microscope can detect, are all provided for within their several spheres of existence. Who then, reflecting upon these things, can imagine that man has no monitor, or that he is hopeless from birth?

"God made us," remarks Adams, "for eternity; and His aim in all He does is to bring us happily to it. Hence the necessity of pain, sickness, crosses, to break the strong chain which binds us to the world, and to force us to take part with God in His grand design."

The voice of conscience is the call of that invisible spiritual intelligence and monitor which *wills* the exercise of the nobler aspirations of the being, leading it upward and onward, while the duty of the material sympathies is to pamper the body and keep it on earth. Between these elements of attraction and repulsion, the soul of man hovers in the body until it is ripened for a new existence in a less material covering in a higher sphere. Watch, then, the voice of conscience in all things, and see that it is preserved void of offence.

Percival, alluding to old age, says that—

"To the intelligent and virtuous, old age presents a scene of tranquil enjoyments, of obedient appetite, of well-regulated affections, of maturity in knowledge, and of calm preparation for immortality. In this serene and dignified state, placed as it were on the confines of two worlds, the mind of a good man reviews what is past with the complacency of an approving conscience in the mercy of God, and with devout aspirations towards His eternal and ever-increasing favour."

> " A venerable aspect !
> Age sits with decent grace upon his visage,
> And worthily become his silver locks :
> He wears the mark of many years well spent,
> Of virtue, truth well tried, and wise experience."—*Rowe.*

The best pulpit efforts have signally failed to remove sectarian differences and jealousies from amongst professing religionists, or to awaken churchgoers from prevailing spiritual indifference. Church governments acknowledge and bemoan the rapid spread of materialistic opinions. These faults rest at their own doors. When " all men are taught of God," as they may be in fact and reality without the teachings of theology or a knowledge of sectarian doctrine, through paid pulpit professors, they will entertain religious beliefs suited to their capacity. Babel, that symbol of the original construction of human laws and religions will be removed, and all will " speak the same ' language,' " *i.e.,* they will have the same religious convictions in degree. It has been those God-dishonouring, contradictory and impossible religious theories of the churches, which have led so many of the best minds of our day either into apathetic indifference as to religious matters, or into those desolate grooves of materialistic thought.

" So, then, because thou art lukewarm, and neither cold nor hot, I will spue thee out of my mouth." " Behold I am at the door and knock, if any man hear my voice and open, . . . I will come in to him, and will sup with him, and he with me."

A pure and simple religion, the truth of which can be demonstrated by the laws of nature and science, is what those minds require, to make of them the brightest, best, and most earnest religionists of the age. Read by the laws of nature, obscure spiritual teachings in Scripture may be understood so as to instruct, edify, and ennoble.

> " See the sole bliss Heaven could on all bestow !
> Which, who but feels, can taste, but thinks can know !
> Yet poor with fortune, and with learning blind,
> The bad must miss, the good untaught will find ;
> Slave to no sect, who takes no private road,
> But looks through nature up to nature's God ;
> Pursues that chain which links the immense design,

> Joins heaven and earth, and mortal and divine ;
> Sees, that no being any bliss can know,
> But touches some above, and some below ;
> Learns, from this union of the rising whole,
> The first, last purpose of the human soul ;
> And knows where faith, laws, morals, all began ;
> All end in love of God, and love of man."—*Pope.*

While churchgoers profess a reliance upon the Scriptures, many will not realise the actuality of such phenomena as are recorded in the second chapter of Acts.   They lose sight of the wonderful sayings and doings of Christ, and the wonderful power which was promised to the disciples. " Verily I say unto you, that whosoever shall say unto this mountain, Be thou removed, and be thou cast into the sea : and shall not doubt in his heart, but shall believe that those things which he saith shall come to pass ; he shall have whatsoever he saith."   These professing Christians, too, make the fearful mistake of assuming that there is no revelation possible now, because, forsooth, in the Revelation of St. John, it is commanded that no man shall add to or take from " the words of the prophecy of this book ;" and they overlook the more rational inference that the words " this book," as they are used, were intended to apply only to this book of Revelation, and that it is obvious that any addition or alteration destroying the meaning of revelation through John or any other inspired channel, would be necessarily wrong, inasmuch as it would be an attempt to foist upon others, as the revelation received through a certain channel, that which was not so actually received through such channel ; but there is no authority whatsoever here for concluding that revelation is closed. In fact, it may be well here to remember that the book of Revelation and the Hebrews, with several of our present New Testament writings, were not generally received as divinely inspired and admitted to a place alongside the four gospels of the New Testament until the third century after Christ.   According to Church history, the *canon* of the gospels was closed about the middle of the second century.   There was no difference of opinion in the churches as to including the four gospels ; and at this time " they began to be regarded as a collection complete in itself, and the exclusive source of information to which the Church appealed." "There was no proof," remarks a writer on the "origin and history of the New Testament," "that the epistles were united together in one collection, much less that they were then classed with the gospels." Some of the books of greatest value, though attributed to apostles, were issued anonymously, such as the gospels of Matthew and John, with the first Epistle of John. Mark and Luke were not only written without the authors' names, but were never supposed to be apostolical writings. This also applied to the Acts. The Epistles of James and Jude, two of the Epistles of John, and the Book of Revelation, were written in names which might or might not be the names of apostles, as there were other disciples named James, Jude, and John." The words assigning the authorship of Revelation to "St. John the Divine," as it appears in our version of the Bible, is an addition of itself, and is only an opinion of the time that John the apostle wrote it. Hebrews was absolutely anonymous, and there never was any agreement as to the writer. The point the churches had to decide upon, then, before they could place these with safety beside the others, was, apart from their apostolic origin or authorship, "Were the writings themselves of such a character that they might be so placed," and this is the way in which all things should be tested. The Book of Revelation, at the commencement of the third century, was not included in the Peshito or Syriac translation made about this time. Eusebius, in his Church History, written about the year 326, divides the collective writings of the Church into three classes, viz.— 1st, the *Homologumena*, which were generally recognised, as constituted, *par excellence*, the New Testament. These were the four gospels, the Acts, and the Epistles of Paul (including Hebrews), the first of John, and the first of Peter. 2d, the *Antilegomena*, or books whose canonical rank was not universally recognised, such as the Epistles of James and Jude, the second Epistle of Peter, and the second and third of John. The Book of Revelation, or the Apocalypse, he did not know where to place, and therefore named it among the books of both the first and second class. In the latter class he placed the Shepherd of Hermas and the Epistle of Barnabas. In the third class he placed the writings forged by heretics, including the gospels of Peter, Thomas, and Matthias, and the Acts of Andrew and

John, which writings were never admitted by the Churches as parts of the New Testament, the *canon* of which, as we now have it, was settled by the Churches in the fourth century.

An authority on the history of religion writes the following sketch, which was published in the year 1782 :—

"The history of religion affords fewer accounts of revolutions, and is more uniform than civil history. The reason of this is plain, for religion is conversant about things which cannot be seen, and which of consequence cannot suddenly and strongly affect the senses of mankind as natural things are apt to do. The invisible nature of spiritual things, the prejudice of habit and of early education, all stand in the way of changes. With regard to the origin of religion, we must have recourse to the Scriptures, and are as necessarily constrained to adopt the account there given as we are to adopt that of creation given in the same books—namely, because no other hath made its appearance which seems in any degree rational or consistent. In what manner the true religion given to Adam was falsified or corrupted by his descendants before the flood doth not clearly appear from Scripture. Idolatry is not mentioned, yet we are assured they were exceedingly wicked; it may be concluded, therefore, that they were either deists or atheists. After the flood idolatry quickly appeared, but what gave rise to it is not certainly known. The origin of idolatry among the Syrians and Arabians, and also in Greece. is accounted for with some probability by the author of 'The Ruins of Balbec' thus—'In those uncomfortable deserts, where day presents nothing to the view but tedious, melancholy prospects of barren sands, the night, for the most part unclouded and serene, discloses a magnificent spectacle to the wondering eye in the host of heaven in all their variety and glory. In the view of this stupendous scene, the transition from admiration to idolatry was too easy to uninstructed minds. The form of idolatry in Greece being different from that of Syria may be attributed to the smiling and variegated scene of mountains, valleys, rivers, woods, groves, and fountains, which the transported imagination supposed to be the seats of invisible deities.' This supposition does not hold good in all cases, for idolatry has not always naturally been produced in the mind of savage, uninstructed man from a view of creation. The Persians of old, and the Moguls in more modern times, are most striking examples, for both these nations were deists, so that other causes must occur, and an imperfect and obscure notion of the true religion seems to be the most probable. Though idolatry, therefore, was formerly very prevalent, it neither extended over the whole earth, nor were the superstitions of idolaters of one kind. Every nation had its respective gods, over which one more excellent than the rest was said to preside, yet in such a manner that this supreme deity himself was controlled by the rigid empire of the fates, or by what philosophers called *eternal necessity.* The gods of the East were different from those of the Gauls, the Germans, and the Northern nations ; and the Grecian divinities differed widely from those of the Egyptians, who deified plants, animals, and a great variety of the productions both of nature and art. Each country, too, had its own particular manner of worshipping and appeasing their respective deities, entirely different from the sacred rites of other countries. As they looked upon the world as one great empire, divided into various provinces, over each of which a certain order of divinities presided, there arose no religious wars or dissensions among the nations, but each suffered its neighbours to follow their own method of worship ; for they imagined that none could behold with contempt the gods of other nations, or force strangers to pay homage to theirs. Although the Romans would not allow any change in the religions publicly professed in the empire, nor any new form of worship to be openly introduced, yet they exercised toleration, for they granted to their citizens full liberty to observe in private the sacred rites of other nations, and to honour foreign deities as they thought proper. The rites and sacrifices observed in honour of the heathen deities were most ridiculous ; and the priests appointed to preside abused their authority by deceiving and imposing upon the people in the grossest manner. From the time of the flood to the coming of Christ, idolatry prevailed among most of the nations of the world ; and although the Jews must be excepted, yet even they were, according to their history in the Old Testament, on all occasions ready to run into it. At the time of Christ's appearance the religion of the Romans, as well as their empire, extended over a great part of the world. Some people there were among the heathens who perceived the absurdities of that system, but being destitute of means, as well as of abilities to effect a reformation, matters went on in their old way. There were various sects of philosophers, yet all proceeded upon false principles, and could therefore be of no service to the advancement or reformation of religion. Nay, some, among whom were the Epicureans and Academics, declared openly against every kind of religion whatever. Two religions at this time flourished in Palestine—viz., the Jewish and Samaritan, between whose respective followers reigned the most violent hatred and contempt. The chief difference between them seems to have been about the place of worship : the Jews would have it to be Jerusalem, and the Samaritans on Mount Gerizim. Though the Jews were right on this point, they had greatly corrupted their religion in other respects. They expected a Saviour, indeed, but they mistook his character, imagining that he was to be a powerful and warlike prince, who should set them free from the Roman yoke, which they bore with the utmost impatience. They also imagined that the whole of religion consisted in observing the rites of Moses, and some others which they had added to them, without the least regard for what is commonly called *morality* or *virtue*, as is evident from the many charges Christ brings against the Pharisees, who had the greatest reputation for sanctity among the whole nation. To these corrupt and vicious principles they added several absurd and superstitious notions concerning the Divine nature, invisible powers, magic, &c., which they had partly imbibed during the Babylonian Captivity, and partly derived from their neighbours in Arabia, Syria, and Egypt. The principal sects among them were the Essenians, Pharisees, and Sadducees. The Samaritans, according to the most general opinion, had corrupted their religion still more than the Jews.

"When the true religion was preached by Jesus, it is not strange he became on that account obnoxious to a people so deeply sunk in corruption and ignorance as the Jews were. The rapid progress of Christianity soon alarmed them, and there was raised various persecutions against its ministers and followers, and the Jews seem at first to have been everywhere the chief promoters of persecution ; for wherever they heard of the increase of the gospel, they officiously went about, and by their calumnies and false suggestions endeavoured to excite the people against the apostles. The heathens, too, although at first they showed no very violent spirit of persecution against the Christians, soon came to hate them as much as the Jews themselves. Tacitus acquaints us with the causes of this hatred when speaking of the first general persecution under Nero ; but his account is so full of downright misrepresentation when he speaks of their ' many and enormous crimes,' without being able to show in what those crimes consisted, it is probable the only reason of this charge against the Christians was their absolute refusal to have any share in the Roman worship, or to countenance the absurd superstitions of paganism in any degree. The persecution under Nero was succeeded by another under Domitian. During the first century Christianity spread considerably ; but as there is no authentic records concerning the travels of the apostles, or the success attending their ministry, it is impossible to determine how far the gospel was carried during this period. We are, however, assured that, even during this early period, many corruptions were creeping in, the progress of which was with difficulty prevented even by the apostles themselves. Some corrupted their profession by a mixture of Judaism, others by mixing it with the oriental philosophy, while others were already attempting to deprive their brethren of liberty, setting themselves up as eminent pastors, in opposition even to the apostles

Hence arose the sects of the Gnostics, Cerinthians, Nicolaitans, Nazarenes, Ebionites, &c., with which the Church was troubled during this century. The ceremonies and method of worship used by the Christians during the first century, as also their church order, government, and discipline, is not ascertained with any degree of exactness. Yet each of those parties which exist at this day contends with the greatest degree of earnestness for that particular mode of worship which they themselves have adopted, and some of the most bigoted would willingly monopolise the word *church* in such a manner as to exclude from all hope of salvation every one who is not attached to their particular party.

" In the second century, Christianity obtained some respite from persecution, which, however, proved very detrimental to its purity. Ceremonies, in themselves futile and useless, but which must be considered as highly pernicious when joined to a religion incapable of any other ornament than the upright lives of its professors, were multiplied only to please the ignorant multitude. The consequence was, that the minds of people were drawn aside from the duties of morality to the observances of idle and unintelligible rites. Mysteries, as they were called, were now also introduced, and the deluded multitude readily imbibed the opinion that, by an observance of these mysteries, they might be exempted from that strict watch over their conduct which the religion of Christ requires. At this time also the clergy began to assume a power over the people very different from that of mere teachers. They persuaded the people that the ministers of the Christian Church succeeded to all the privileges of the Jewish priesthood, and accordingly the bishops considered themselves as invested with a rank and character similar to those of the high-priest among the Jews, while the presbyters represented the priests, and the deacons the Levites. This notion, which was first introduced in the reign of Adrian, proved the source of very considerable honour and profit to the clergy. The form of ecclesiastical government was in this century rendered permanent and uniform. One inspector or bishop presided over each Christian assembly, to which office he was elected by the voices of the whole people. To assist him in his office he formed a council of presbyters, which was not confined to any stated number. To the bishops and presbyters the ministers, or *deacons*, were subject ; and the latter were divided into a variety of classes, as the different emergencies of the Church required. During a great part of this century the churches were independent of each other ; nor were they joined together by association, confederacy, or any other bonds but those of charity. Each assembly was a little state government by its own laws, which were enacted, or at least approved of, by the society. But in process of time, all the Christian churches of a province were formed into one large ecclesiastical body, which, like confederated states, assembled at certain times, in order to deliberate about the common interests of the whole. This institution had its origin among the Greeks; but in a short time it became universal, and similar assemblies were formed in all places where the gospel had been planted. These assemblies, which consisted of the deputies or commissioners from several churches, were called *synods* by the Greeks, and *councils* by the Latins; and the laws enacted in these general meetings were called *canons, i.e., rules*. These councils, of which we find not the smallest trace before the middle of this century, changed the whole face of the Church, and gave it a new form; for by them the ancient privileges of the people were considerably diminished, and the power and authority of the bishops greatly augmented. The humility, indeed, and prudence of these pious prelates hindered them from assuming all at once the power with which they were afterwards invested. At their first appearance in these general councils, they acknowledged that they were no more than the delegates of their respective churches, and that they acted in the name and by the appointment of their people. But they soon changed this humble tone; imperceptibly extended the limits of their authority; turned their influence into dominion, their counsels into laws; and at length openly asserted that Christ had empowered them to prescribe to His people *authoritative rules of faith* and *manners*. Another effect of these councils was the gradual abolition of that perfect equality which reigned among all bishops in the primitive times. For the order and decency of these assemblies required that some one of the provincial bishops met in council should be invested with a superior degree of power and authority, and hence the rights of metropolitans derive their origin. In the meantime, the bounds of the Church were enlarged; the custom of holding councils was followed wherever the sound of the gospel had reached; and the universal Church had now the appearance of one vast republic formed by a combination of a great number of little states. This occasioned the creation of a new order of ecclesiastics, who were appointed in different parts of the world as heads of the Church, and whose offices it was to preserve the consistence and union of that immense body, whose members were so widely dispersed throughout the nations. Such was the nature and office of the *patriarchs;* among whom, at length, ambition, being arrived at its most insolent period, formed a new dignity, investing the bishop of Rome with the title and authority of the *prince of the patriarchs*. During this second century all the sects continued which had sprung up in the first, with the addition of several others, the most remarkable of which were the *Ascetics*. These owed their rise to some doctors of the Church, who asserted that

Christ had established *a double rule of sanctity and virtue* for two different orders of Christians. Of these rules, one was ordinary, the other extraordinary; the one of a lower dignity, the other more sublime; the first for persons in the active scenes of life, the other for those who, in sacred retreat, aspired after the glory of a celestial state. In consequence of this system, they divided into two parts all those moral doctrines and instructions which they had received either by writing or tradition. One of these divisions they called *precepts*, and the other *counsels*. They gave the name of *precepts* to those laws that were universally obligatory upon all orders of men; and that of *counsels* to those which related to Christians of more sublime rank, who proposed to themselves great and glorious ends, and breathed after an intimate communion with the Supreme Being. Thus were produced all at once a new sect of men who made pretensions to uncommon sanctity and virtue, and declared their resolution of obeying all the precepts and counsels of Christ, in order to their enjoyment of communion with God here; and also that, after the dissolution of their mortal bodies, they might ascend to Him with the greater facility, and find nothing to retard their approach to the centre of happiness and perfection. They looked upon themselves as prohibited from the use of things which it was lawful for other Christians to enjoy, such as wine, flesh, matrimony, and commerce. They thought it their indispensable duty to attenuate their body by watchings, abstinence, labour, and hunger. They looked for felicity in solitary retreats and desert places; where by severe and assiduous efforts of sublime meditation, they raised the soul above all external objects, and all sensual pleasures. They were distinguished from other Christians not only by their title of *Ascetics* and philosophers, but also by their garb. In this century, indeed, those who embraced such a kind of life submitted themselves to all those mortifications in private, without breaking asunder those social bands, or without withdrawing themselves from mankind; but in process of time they retired into desert places, and, after the example of the Essenes and Therapeutæ, they formed themselves into certain companies. People joined this sect, however, who laboured under an opinion which has been more or less prevalent in all ages and in all countries, namely, that religion consists more in ceremonies and prayers than in fulfilling the social duties of life. Nothing can be more evident than that the Scripture reckons the fulfilling of these infinitely superior to the observance of all the ceremonies that can be imagined—yet it somehow or other happens that almost everybody is more inclined to observe the ceremonial part of devotion than the moral; and hence, according to the different humours or constitutions of different people, there have been numberless forms of Christianity, and the most virulent contentions among those who professed themselves followers of the Prince of Peace. The tendency of those who attached themselves to the Ascetics was to introduce Jewish and other superstitions and ceremonials, and to set up human traditions and rules as standards for their general spiritual guidance ; and instead of a humble submission of the human to the Divine will, and the consequent enjoyment of a sublime Divine communion, they afflicted themselves with mutterings of long prayers and with meaningless ceremonials, blindly leaning upon the stated traditionary efficacy of sacrificial laws in its Christianised form, meaning 'the blood of the Lamb.' The errors of the Ascetics did not stop here, for, in compliance with the doctrines of some pagan philosophers, they affirmed that it was not only lawful, but even praiseworthy to deceive, and to use the expedient of a lie, in order to advance the cause of piety and truth ; and hence the *pious frauds* for which the Church of Rome hath been so notorious, and with which she hath been so often and justly reproached. As Christians deviated more from the true practice of their religion, they became more zealous of the external profession of it. Anniversary festivals were celebrated to commemorate the death and resurrection of Christ, and of the effusion of the Holy Ghost on the apostles. There arose, indeed, violent contests concerning the days on which these festivals were to be kept. The Asiatic churches differed in this point from those of Europe ; and towards the end of the century, Victor, Bishop of Rome, determined upon forcing the eastern churches to follow the rules laid down by the western ones. They, however, absolutely refused to comply, and thereupon Victor cut them off from communion with the Church at Rome, but, by the intercession of some prudent people, the difference was made up for the present.

"During most of the third century, the Christians enjoyed their religion with little molestation ; though the emperors Maximinus and Decius made them feel all the rigours of a severe persecution. Their reigns, however, were but short, and from the time of Decius to that of Diocletian, the professors of Christianity were not molested. Then, indeed, they suffered a terrible persecution for ten years from Diocletian and Galerius, but they found an asylum in the dominions of Constantius.

"In the reign of Constantine, in the fourth century, the Christian religion was established by law throughout the Roman empire. This event, however, so favourable to the outward peace of the Church, was far from promoting its internal harmony, or the reformation of its leaders. The clergy, who had all this time been augmenting their power at the expense of the liberty of the people, now set no bounds to their ambition. The Bishop of Rome was the first in rank, and distinguished by a sort of pre-eminency above the rest of the prelates. He surpassed all his brethren in the magnificence and splendour of the church over which he presided; in the riches of his revenues and possessions; in the number and variety of his ministers; in his credit with the people, and in his sumptuous and splendid manner of living. Hence it happened that when a new pontiff was to be chosen by the presbyters and people, the city of Rome was generally agitated with dissensions, tumults, and cabals, which often produced fatal consequences. The intrigues and disturbances which prevailed in that city in the year 366, when, upon the death of Liberius, another pontiff was to be chosen in his place, are a sufficient proof of what we have advanced. Upon that occasion one faction elected Damasus to that high dignity; while the opposite party chose Urficinus, a deacon of the vacant church, to succeed Liberius. This double election gave rise to a dangerous schism, and to a sort of civil war within the city of Rome, which was carried on with the utmost barbarity and fury, and produced the most cruel massacres and desolations. The inhuman contest ended in the victory of Damasus; but whose cause was most just it is hard to determine. Notwithstanding the pomp and splendour which surrounded the Roman see, it is certain that the bishops of Rome had not yet acquired that pre-eminence of power and jurisdiction which they afterwards enjoyed. In the ecclesiastical commonwealth, indeed, they were the most eminent order of citizens, but still they were citizens as well as their brethren, and subject, like them, to the laws and edicts of the emperors. All religious causes of extraordinary importance were examined and determined, either by judges appointed by the emperors, or in councils assembled for that purpose; while those of inferior moment were decided in each district by its respective bishop. The ecclesiastical laws were enacted either by the emperor or councils. None of the bishops acknowledged that they derived their authority from the permission and appointment of the Bishop of Rome, or that they were created bishops by the favour of the *apostolic see*. On the contrary, they all maintained that they were the ambassadors and ministers of Jesus Christ, and that their authority was derived from above. It must, however, be observed that, even in this century, several of those steps were laid by which the Bishops of Rome mounted afterwards to the summit of ecclesiastical power and despotism. This happened partly by the imprudence of the emperors, partly by the dexterity of the Roman prelates themselves, and partly by the inconsiderate zeal and precipitate judgment of certain bishops. The imprudence of the emperor and precipitation of the bishops were remarkably discovered in the following event, which favoured extremely the ambition of the Roman pontiff. About the year 372, Valentinian enacted a law empowering the Bishop of Rome to examine and judge other

E

bishops, that religious disputes might not be decided by any profane or secular judges. The bishops, assembled in council at Rome in 378, not considering the fatal consequences that must arise from this imprudent law both to themselves and to the Church, declared their approbation in the strongest terms, and recommended the execution of it in their address to the Emperor Gratian. Some think, indeed, that this law empowered the Roman bishop to judge only the bishops within the limits of his jurisdiction; others that his power was given only for a certain time, and for a particular purpose. This last notion seems the most probable; but still this privilege must have been an excellent instrument in the hands of sacerdotal ambition. By the removal of the seat of empire to Constantinople, the emperor raised up, in the bishop of this new metropolis, a formidable opponent to the Bishop of Rome, and a bulwark which threatened a vigorous opposition to his growing authority. For as the emperor, in order to render Constantinople a second Rome, enriched it with all the rights and privileges, honours and ornaments of the ancient capital of the world, so its bishop, measuring his own dignity and rank by the magnificence of the new city, and its eminence as the residence of the emperor, assumed an equal degree of dignity with the Bishop of Rome, and claimed a superiority over the rest of the episcopal order. Nor did the emperors disapprove of these high pretensions, since they considered their own dignity as connected in a certain measure with that of the bishop of their imperial city. Accordingly, in a council held at Constantinople in the year 381, by the authority of Theodosius the Great, the bishop of that city was, during the absence of the Bishop of Alexandria, and against the consent of the Roman prelate, placed by the third canon of that council in the first rank after the Bishop of Rome, and consequently above those of Alexandria and Antioch. Nectarius was the first bishop who enjoyed these new honours accumulated upon the see of Constantinople. His successor, the celebrated John Chrysostom, extended still further the privileges of that see, and submitted to its jurisdiction all Thrace, Asia, and Pontus; nor were the succeeding bishops of that imperial city destitute of a fervent zeal to augment their privileges and extend their dominion. By this unexpected promotion the most disagreeable effects were produced. The Bishops of Alexandria were not only filled with the most inveterate hatred against those of Constantinople, but a contention was excited between the Bishops of Rome and Constantinople, which, after being carried on for many ages, concluded at last in the separation of the Greek and Latin Churches. From this period the Christian Church set no bounds to its corruptions; and while the essence of it was totally lost in the West among a heap of idle ceremonies, the very name was exterminated in the East by the Mahometans, who with amazing celerity overran Asia and Africa, carrying along and establishing their religion wherever they went.

"In the beginning of the seventh century, according to the most learned historians, Boniface III. engaged Phocas, Emperor of Constantinople, to take from the bishop of that metropolis the title of *œcumenical* or universal bishop, and to confer it upon the Roman pontiff; and thus was first introduced the supremacy of the Pope. The Roman pontiffs used all methods to maintain and enlarge this authority and pre-eminence, which they had acquired from one of the most odious tyrants that ever disgraced the annals of history. It would be endless to recount all the enormities and superstitions with which the world was now filled under the name of religion. Excommunications now received that infernal power which dissolved all connections, so that those whom the bishops or their chief excluded from the church-communion were disgraced to a level with the beasts. The Roman pontiffs continued to increase their power by every kind of artifice and fraud which can dishonour the heart of man; and, by continually taking advantage of the civil dissensions which reigned in Italy, France, and Germany, their power in civil affairs arose at last to an enormous height. The clergy were immersed in crimes of the deepest dye; and the laity, imagining themselves able to purchase pardon of their sins for money, followed the examples of their pastors without remorse. Devotees and reputed saints, on the other hand, were led into the absurd error that religion consisted in acts of austerity; they lived in the most ridiculous way among wild beasts, ran naked through lonely deserts with a furious aspect and all the agitations of frenzy, prolonged their wretched life by grass and wild herbs, avoided the sight and conversation of men, remained motionless in certain places for several years exposed to the inclemency of the seasons, and finally, towards the end of their lives, shut themselves up in narrow and miserable huts—all this being considered true piety, and an acceptable method of worshipping the Deity and attaining a share in His favour.

"In this manner matters went on till the beginning of the sixteenth century, when the Roman pontiffs lived in the utmost tranquillity; nor had they, according to appearances at that time, any reason to fear opposition to their authority in any respect, since the commotions raised by the Waldenses, Albigenses, &c., were now entirely suppressed. Notwithstanding this apparent tranquillity, it must not be concluded that their measures were universally applauded. Not only private persons, but also the most powerful princes and sovereign states, exclaimed loudly against the tyranny of the popes, and the unbridled licentiousness of the clergy of all denominations. They demanded, therefore, a reformation of the Church in its head and members, and a general council to accomplish that necessary purpose

But these complaints and demands were not carried to such a length as to produce any good effect; since they came from persons who never entertained the least doubt about the superior authority of the Pope in religious matters, and who of consequence, instead of attempting themselves to bring about that reformation which was so ardently desired, remained entirely inactive, or looked for redress to the Court of Rome, or to a general council. A single person, Martin Luther, a monk of the order of St. Augustine, ventured to oppose himself to the whole torrent of papal power and despotism. This bold attempt was first made public on the 30th September 1517; and notwithstanding all the efforts of the Pope and his adherents, the doctrines of Luther continued daily to gain ground. Others, encouraged by his success, lent their assistance in the work of reformation; which at last produced new Churches, founded upon principles quite different from that of Rome, and which still continue. The ecclesiastical government of the Papacy has employed many volumes in describing it. The cardinals, who are next in dignity to his Holiness, are seventy, but that number is seldom or never complete: they are appointed by the Pope, who takes care to have a majority of Italian cardinals, that the chair may not be removed from Rome, as it was once to Avignon in France, the then Pope being a Frenchman. In promoting foreign prelates to the cardinalship, the Pope regulates himself according to the nominations of the princes who profess that religion. His chief minister is the cardinal patron, generally his nephew, or near relation, who improves the time of the Pope's reign by amassing what he can. When met in a consistory, the cardinals pretend to control the Pope in matters both spiritual and temporal, and have been sometimes known to prevail. The reign of a Pope is seldom of long duration, being generally old men at the time of their election. The conclave is a scene where the cardinals principally endeavour to display their parts, and where many transactions pass which hardly show proof of their inspiration from the Holy Ghost. During the election of a Pope in 1721 the animosities ran so high that they came to blows with both their hands and feet, and threw the ink-standishes at each other. We shall here give an extract from the creed of Pope Pius IV., 1560, before his elevation to the chair, which contains the principal points wherein the Church of Rome differs from the Protestant Churches. After declaring his belief in one God, and other heads wherein Christians in general are agreed, he proceeds as follows :—

"'I most firmly admit and embrace the apostolical and ecclesiastical traditions, and all other constitutions of the same Church. I do admit the Holy Scriptures in the same sense that the holy Mother Church doth, whose business it is to judge of the true sense and interpretation of them; and I will interpret them according to the unanimous consent of the fathers. I do profess and believe that there are seven sacraments of the law, truly and properly so called, instituted by Jesus Christ our Lord, and necessary to the salvation of mankind, though not all of them to every one ; namely, baptism, confirmation, eucharist, penance, extreme unction, orders, and marriage, and that they do confer grace ; and that of these, baptism, confirmation, and orders, may not be repeated without sacrilege. I do also receive and admit the received rites of the Catholic Church in her solemn administration of the above said sacraments. I do embrace and receive all and every thing that hath been defined and declared by the holy Council of Trent concerning original sin and justification.' [The Council of Trent was a convocation of Roman Catholic divines, who assembled at Trent, by virtue of a bull from the Pope in 1546, to determine upon certain points of faith, and to suppress what they were pleased to term the rising heretics of the Church.] ' I do also profess that in the mass there is offered unto God a true, proper, and propitiatory sacrifice for the quick and the dead ; and that in the most holy sacrament of the eucharist there is truly, really, and substantially, the body and blood, together with the soul and divinity of our Lord Jesus Christ ; and that there is a conversion made of the whole substance of the bread into the body, and of the whole substance of the wine into the blood, which conversion the Catholic Church calls Transubstantiation. I confess that, under one kind only, whole and entire, Christ and a true sacrament is taken and received. I do firmly believe that there is a purgatory ; and that the souls kept prisoners there do receive help by the suffrages of the faithful: I do likewise believe that the saints reigning together with Christ are to be worshipped and prayed unto ; and that they do offer prayers unto God for us, and that their relics are to be had in veneration. I do most firmly assert that the images of Christ, of the blessed Virgin, the mother of God, and of other saints, ought to be had and retained, and that due honour and veneration ought to be given unto them. I do likewise affirm that the power of indulgence was left by Christ to the Church, and that the use of them is very beneficial to Christian people.*

---

* A long list of indulgences, or fees of the Pope's chancery, may be seen in a book printed about 243 years ago, by the authority of the then Pope. It has been translated into English, under the title of ' Rome a great Custom-house for Sin ;' from which we shall give a few extracts :—

ABSOLUTIONS.

For him that stole holy or consecrated things out of a holy place, 10s. 6d.

For him who lays with a woman in a church, 9s.

For a layman for *murdering* a layman, 7s. 6d.

I do acknowledge the holy, catholic, and apostolical Roman Church to be the mother and mistress of all Churches ; and I do promise and swear true obedience to the Bishop of Rome, the successor of St. Peter, the prince of the apostles, and vicar of Jesus Christ. I do undoubtedly receive and profess all other things, which have been delivered, defined, and declared by the sacred canons and œcumenical councils, and especially by the holy Synod of Trent. And all other things contrary thereto, and all heresies condemned, rejected, and anathematised by the Church, I do likewise condemn, reject, and anathematise.' "

To return, it may be said that for religious teachers to attempt to deny ever-open revelation to man, and to pro-

---

For him that *killeth* his father, mother, wife, or sister, 10s. 6d.

For laying violent hands on a *clergyman*, so it be without effusion of blood, 10s. 6d.

For a priest that keeps a concubine ; as also his dispensation for being irregular, 10s. 6d.

For him that lyeth with his *own mother, sister,* or *godmother,* 7s. 6d.

For him that *burns* his neighbour's house, 12s.

For him that forgeth the Pope's hand, £1, 7s.

For him that forgeth letters apostolical, £1, 7s.

For him that takes two holy orders in one day, £2, 6s.

For a king for going to the holy sepulchre without licence, £7, 10s.

DISPENSATIONS.

For a bastard to enter all holy orders, 18s.

For a man or woman that is found hanged, that they may have Christian burial, £1, 7s. 6d.

LICENCES.

For a layman to change his vow of going to Rome to visit the apostolic churches, 18s.

To eat flesh and white meats in Lent, and other fasting days, 10s. 6d.

That a king or queen shall enjoy such indulgences as if they went to Rome, £15.

For a queen to adopt a child, £300.

To marry in times prohibited, £2, 5s.

To eat flesh in times prohibited, £1, 4s.

Not to be tied to fasting days, £1, 4s.

For a town to take out of a church them (murderers) that have taken sanctuary therein, £4, 10s.

FACULTIES.

To absolve all delinquents, £3.

To dispense with irregularities, £3."

mulgate such teaching openly, is a species of tyranny equally dastardly to any attempt to shut up in constant darkness and deny him light, life, progression, and expression, which are the common heritage of all God's creatures. Yet, this tyranny has been, and is still exerted over men's minds, to debar them from the exercise of that inherent quality, by which alone the spiritually famished may truly be satisfied, and the soul may be expanded. The whole superstructure of all that is good and true in Scripture, is based upon the ever-existing law in nature by which revelations are made ; and to rob the spiritually-minded of ever-open revelation would be like eclipsing a lighthouse to the mariner as he was nearing port on a dark night.

The religion as well as the language of a people affords a pretty correct indication of their condition of mind. The conceptions formed of Deity are more or less perfect according to the liberality, the goodness, and the intelligence of the people. Those minds that were capable of "receiving" the lofty spiritual truths which fell from the lips of Jesus were no longer content with the use of the material symbols of the Mosaic dispensation. "Whom say ye that I am ? " asked Jesus of Peter, whose reply was, "Thou art Christ, the Son of the living God." Then said he, "Flesh and blood hath not revealed it unto thee, but my Father who is in heaven." So is it with scriptural truths and religion at the present time. No mind can realise the truth which does not yearn for it, and thus attract it. It is not forced upon us, nor can flesh and blood, with fear of hell-fire, reveal it to us; but if we desire it, we can realise it through our own experiences. "Blessedness," said Richter, "is a whole eternity, older than damnation."

Man by his experiences must feel a want of the divine spirit, that heavenly food, wherewith to satisfy the cravings of his higher nature, and to bring to him a happiness beyond that of the mere unsatisfying gratifications of the material desires, before his mind or soul can be expected to attract such spiritual happiness. The soul or mind must be perfected according to the natural law of attraction and repulsion, by the purity and constancy of the desires and actions—the ripening of mind for a higher condition of existence than that represented in the material body must be gradual. In other words, while "conversion" may be a sudden experience, a bursting forth into existence of a want not before fully realised, and may therefore be regarded as an entrance on a new path in life, "reform" and godly character are a matter of time, and must grow naturally out of the exercise of pure earnest desire and well-doing. Let him who would be a Christian and a good man go about it according to the most approved way which has been disclosed to the mind of man. Let him go to a phrenologist of ability and get his head examined—let him study by every other means within his power his faults, and let him studiously endeavour to check them. Let him be ever watchful of the cravings of his worldly "self," which will be continuously presenting themselves in a thousand plausible forms, but which must be always conquered. "Every man," remarks Sir J. Stevens, "has in himself a continent of undiscovered character. Happy is he who acts the Columbus to his own soul." Let him remember that if his leading desire through life is to be instrumental in doing general good, and that if he sinks "self" in the interests of others, and if his innermost thoughts be kept free from revengeful feeling and pure in other respects, his earthly tabernacle may thus be built up a fit abiding-place for Divine Influence, and he may receive through it that unerring guidance which, when implicitly followed, leads unfailingly to lasting success and genuine happiness. The thoughts and desires make the man—and as "the tree is known by its fruits," so may the character of a man be discovered by the influences for good or evil which grow out of his sayings and doings, as these in themselves are but the expression of his inmost thoughts and desires. Jeremy Taylor remarks that—

"A pure mind in a chaste body is the mother of wisdom and deliberation, sober counsels and ingenuous actions, open deportment and sweet carriage, sincere principles and unprejudicate understanding, love of God and self-denial, peace and confidence, holy prayers and spiritual comfort, and a pleasure of spirit infinitely greater than the sottish pleasure of unchastity."

> "So dear to Heaven is saintly chastity,
> That when a soul is found sincerely so,
> A thousand liveried angels lacquey her,
> Driving far off each thing of sin and guilt,

And in clear dream, and solemn vision,
Tell her of things that no gross ear can hear ;
Till oft converse with heavenly visitants,
Begin to cast and teem on the outward shape,
The unpolluted temple of the mind,
And turn it by degrees to the soul's essence,
Till all be made immortal."—*Milton.*

Every night review the thoughts and doings of the day, examining carefully and honestly, without reserve, all short-comings. Earnestly desire divine assistance to overcome wherein you have failed, and exert your best efforts, and assuredly an amendment will follow, although it may appear slow. In cases of doubt seek divine light, and strive for it, and it will come. Do unto others as you might wish others to do unto you—let this golden rule guide you, if you hesitate as to how to treat a fellow-being. Be guided in your thoughts and actions more by the inward voice and a knowledge of natural law than by any external direction, even though it be presented on the highest external authority ; for authority forbids the exercise of reason, it is at variance with the immutable laws of nature, and it endeavours to frustrate appeal to inward conscience.

Above many things, beware of nursing anger and revenge.

"What a chain of evils," said St. Ephraim, "does that man prepare for himself who is a slave to anger ! He is the murderer of his own soul, yea, to the letter he is so, for he lives in a continual torment. He is devoured by an inward fire, and his body partakes of his sufferings. Terror reigns around the passionate man—he is alike odious to God and man, and is insupportable even to himself."

"To be angry about trifles," says Watts, "is mean and childish; to rage and be furious is brutish; and to maintain perpetual wrath is akin to the practice and temper of devils ; but to prevent and suppress rising resentment is wise and glorious, is manly and divine."

Confucius said, "When anger rises, think of the consequences." "When I myself had twice or thrice made a resolute resistance unto anger," remarked Plutarch, "the like befell me that did the Thebans; who having once foiled the Lacedæmonians (who before that time had held themselves invincible), never after lost so much as one battle which they fought against them."

In Proverbs we have it very wisely put, "He that governeth his own temper is stronger than he that taketh a city." "The sun,"

says Colton, "should not set upon our anger, neither should he
rise upon our confidence. We should freely forgive, but forget
rarely. I will not be revenged, and this I owe to my enemy; but
I will remember, and this I owe to myself."

To give way to anger and to nurse revenge is to kindle
a consuming fire within ourselves which destroys alike body
and soul—to yield to anger, like yielding to any other
passion or evil inclination, is followed by a weakening of
the natural capacity of overcoming that evil when next
overtaken by it. To quench within us passionate feelings
arising from a wrong sustained is like rescuing our dwelling-
house from an incendiary fire ; besides, it improves and
strengthens our mind-capacity of dealing with and resisting
future trials, and enables us better to consider and deal
with those difficult positions in which we so often find ourselves placed in the midst of excitement. If the physiology
of unseen influences were better understood, or, in other
words, if it were not for indifference and ignorance being so
general upon such matters, the "sin" or organic injury
occasioned by anger and revenge, as well as many other
evils, might be overcome. The depth of the philosophy in
many of the teachings of Jesus has not yet been explored.
If, for instance, a person acts in accordance with the teachings of Jesus, and renders good for evil, he is actually the
gainer, inasmuch as his mind being calm he is fitted to act
wisely ; and not only is this the case, but his physical organism, like a well-tuned instrument, may be harmoniously
acted upon and impressed more clearly by pure unseen
intelligences, if his desire be to do the will of the Father.
On the other hand, if wrong, violence, or passion be requited
in turn by angry passions and revengeful feelings, both
minds being in affinity are (without their cognisance) attracted towards the other, and the material organism of
each is likely to be impressed not only by other evil unseen
intelligences attracted, but it is likely to be possessed or
acted upon by the invisible mind-influence of his opponent,
and while each imagines that he is fighting against his
adversary, he is in reality fighting against himself, so that
practically—all other things being equal—he who has the
strongest will to do the most injury to his opponent is he
who will sustain the greatest injury himself. Thus wisely
ordered are the laws of nature to protect the weak against

the strong, and to teach us consideration for our fellow-creatures—the law of love, and the at-one-ment of mankind. Mr. St. John very truly observes that—

"Few men die of age. Almost all die of disappointment, passions mental or bodily, or toil, or accident. The passions kill men sometimes even suddenly. The common expression, choked with passion, has little exaggeration in it; for even though not suddenly fatal, strong passions shorten life. Strong-bodied men often die young—weak men live longer than the strong, for the strong use their strength, and the weak have none to use. The latter take care of themselves; the former do not. As it is with the body, so it is with the mind and temper. The strong are apt to break, or, like the candle, to run; the weak burn out. The inferior animals, which live, in general, regular and temperate lives, have generally their prescribed term of years. The horse lives twenty-five years; the ox fifteen to twenty; the lion about twenty; the dog ten or twelve; the rabbit eight; the guinea-pig six or seven years. These numbers all bear a similar proportion to the time the animal takes to grow its full size. But man, of all the animals, is the one that seldom comes up to this standard of age. He ought to live one hundred years, according to this physiological law, for five times twenty are one hundred; but instead of this he scarcely reaches, on the average, four times his growing period—while the cat lives six times, and the rabbit lives even eight times this standard of measurement. The reason is obvious—man is not only the most irregular and the most intemperate, but the most laborious and hard-worked of all animals. He is also the most irritable of all animals; and there is reason to believe, though we cannot tell what an animal secretly feels, that, more than any other animal, man cherishes wrath to keep it warm, and consumes himself with the fire of his own secret reflections."

Much confusion of thought arises from the employment in language of words which when closely analysed convey no possible meaning. The use of the words "supernatural" and "miracle," for instance, should now be quite obsolete, as they are wholly inappropriate for present use in expressing the religion of Christ, or the religious beliefs of the more enlightened minds of the present time. God is the God of nature, and nothing can be supernatural or above nature which is in nature. An occurrence which could not be explained by any law of nature known to those who witnessed it, used to be called "miraculous," although it must necessarily have been done by some natural, although, as in Christ's case, some may hold, superhuman power ; but there is no more necessity for maintaining that the inspiration claimed for Jesus' teachings is proved by his miracles than there is for believing that any clever conjurer is inspired. The correctness of using the word " superhuman," when referring to the so-called miracles of Jesus, even, is very doubtful, for, admitting the account of the miraculous feeding of the multitude with loaves and fishes, for instance, as truthful, and that we have no knowledge of the laws of nature (if not by electro-biology) by which it was performed, are we justified in assuming that it was even superhuman, when we consider it in the light of the following words attributed to Jesus, also taken as truthful ? " He that believeth on me, the works that I do shall he do also ; and greater works than these shall he do ; because I go unto my Father. And whatsoever ye shall ask in my name, that will I do, that the Father may be glorified in the Son." By this light, it would be hard to define what general limit, if any, can be put to the powers which may be exercised through a human being ; and it does not get rid of the difficulty to simply acknowledge that the exercise of the greatest as well as the smallest powers must of necessity be through the instrumentality of divinely-established laws in nature—although this establishes that nothing can be " supernatural " in the strict sense of the word. As " a good tree is known by its fruit," so do we recognise in the lesson of Christ's life and his teachings the excellence of an inspired nature. It is immaterial when or by whom the Gospels were written. In the writings themselves is found the best evidence of their general worth. Inspiration or revelation from unseen intelligence as an actuality can be realised and testified to by some minds at the present time, through the knowledge they have attained, by means of it, of the existence of certain laws in nature rendering it practicable ; and the fact of having received revelations themselves by such means as coincide in their process of action with those laws further tends to establish the actuality of such invisible laws. While all spiritual aspirations should undoubtedly be directed to the very highest conceptions of Divinity which the mind is capable of realising, it is impossible for man to say whether or not the revelations he may receive are actually divine or through finite spirit-agencies. Nothing living is too small or too big, we believe, to be controlled and cared for under those laws, which, conceived in perfect wisdom, cannot go wrong ; and the mind may believe in the existence of an invisible God spirit or mind pervading and governing all space and matter, not only of this earth which we inhabit, but throughout all those countless systems of worlds revolving in supposed limitless space. Yet man receives communications from departed friends of things which are believed to be known only by them, and such departed ones invariably testify that they have not yet seen God, although they testify that they can see more than we do of the infinite beauty of God's universe. There is no reason, that we are aware of, why departed friends in the spirit-world should see God, any more than there is reason why we in this material existence should see God, further than He is revealed to us in His beautiful laws and works in nature. If a person had to travel through a wild country, and he discovered, as he proceeded, that all his wants had been anticipated and supplies were always at hand, but that the donor left no traces of his presence or personality, the best evidence would remain to establish first, The foresight ; and second, The genuine disinterested love and beneficence of the giver. The greatest blemish upon all the great and noble works of man is the evidences they bear of self-glorification, leading to man - worship. Because God is not a visible personality to us in the material world, and because it is generally and reasonably supposed that the powers of observation of intelligences in the spirit-world are very much enlarged, it is therefore assumed by some that immediately after leaving the material body, they may see God. If these persons, however, will accept the theory that mind expresses itself, according to its condition, through the various forms of matter, they may probably come to understand better what an intense sublimate essence the centre of government of the Almighty, All-wise, All-pervading, and All-loving must represent, and how very material high spiritual intelligences must appear in contrast, and how difficult it must be for them to distinguish, or in other words, " look upon the face of God." Taken in this light, it would be more reasonable to suppose that man in the earth-life should see his friends departed

to spirit-life—for they are to all intents the same condition of mind—than that such departed ones could see the
Supreme Being, whose mind is the perfection of sublimity.
Returning to the subject, as to Divine Revelation, although
man receives revelations from unseen spiritual intelligence
in various forms, still there is no evidence to us of *direct
divine revelation*, nor does it appear necessary that the
finite mind should receive direct divine revelation beyond
what it receives by natural law constantly through its individual spiritual intelligence or conscience, which itself is
animated by divine will, directly as well as indirectly,
through departed spirit-friends or guardian angels.   On
the other hand, there is nothing to disprove that many of
the revelations received from unseen spiritual intelligence
are actually Divine revelations received from the all-pervading governing mind of the universe.   If every thought
and action of individuals be known to the all-pervading
mind, and may be likewise witnessed by spirit-friends, it is
illogical to say that information received from unseen intelligence of occurrences which were known to perhaps one
man alone in the body, can only therefore come from the
spiritual intelligence of that one man, if dead, for it might
either come from other observant but unseen individual
spirit-witnesses, or from the God-mind itself, whether as
a witness, or whether the individual mind of the person
deceased, with all its acquired experiences, had been
absorbed into and become part of the God-mind.   It is
impossible to imagine when or at what stage of existence
the individuality or identity of mind itself ceases, *i.e.*, when
it may be so refined as to be absorbed into the central
mind ; whether it ever becomes so absorbed; or whether
the mind of man must necessarily pass through such stages
of existence as spirit, angel, archangel, and of those still
more exalted spiritual beings called Gods (who are supposed to be commissioned with the destiny of worlds), absorb-
ing in each of these existences additional experiences before
it is itself absorbed in the God-mind.   It is, however,
obvious that one great indispensable lesson has to be
thoroughly acquired before the mind can be absorbed, and
that is the lesson of total and complete self-abnegation.
All the cherished concerns of the individual must be brought
into subjection by a leading desire to conform in all things

to the will of the Father, before the real aim of existence—
that at-one-ment—that great leading precept and example
of Jesus' life—can be accomplished. As particles, in affinity,
tend to fly together and corporate—as insects, beasts, birds,
and fishes, and all kinds of animal life, associate in swarms,
in herds, in flocks, and shoals, under a leading intelligence—as sexes unite—as individuals of the same general
dispositions generally associate together—as savages unite
in tribes, and civilised people unite in nations and districts
for general government purposes—the tendency throughout nature, in the material life, is therefore seen to be association, and the tendency in the spiritual life may therefore
also fairly be presumed to be association or incarnation, or
in other words, the union of intelligences that are in affinity. It will thus be seen that the more the one grand law
of at-one-ment, under the will of God, prevails amongst intelligences, the sooner will the Church of Christ be gathered
and harvested, in one great and glorious whole, into the
kingdom of the Father, and the highest aim of individual
minds will be realised, in their being thus absorbed and
made joint partners with Him in glory.

There are supposed to be three stages of existence—in
man, spirit, and angel. In each of these, the education,
from experiences acquired, must be completed before a
higher condition can be reached. The change of existence
from body to spirit is called death. If the body-education
is not completed the spirit returns to body again, and it is
only when it is sufficiently ripened to be harvested that the
final "resurrection" or after death or passage from spirit
to perfected spirit or angel takes place. Man, while in the
body, gains his experiences of the married state, and has an
opportunity afforded him of growing into affinity in body
and mind with woman. In the spirit state—freed from
the body—they remain as man and woman, but are freed
from the material proclivities of the body; and in this
condition, if they prove to be in perfect affinity of mind,
thus freed from their grosser natures, and are otherwise
ripened for a higher state of existence, they being thus
proved " at one," are absorbed into each other, in the final
resurrection, as one perfected spirit or angel, and they being
one, are from thence freed from all sexual distinctions.
[Luke xx. 34–36, " The children of this world marry.

But they which shall be accounted worthy to obtain that world, and the resurrection from the dead, neither marry nor are given in marriage. Neither can they die any more : for they are equal unto the angels ; and are the children of God, being the children of the resurrection."]

Turning now to the material condition of man and its education on earth, we find that the growth and expansion of the human mind has often been retarded by a stifling of the free expression of honest independent convictions. In religious and political concerns, a spirit of toleration happily reigns at the present time which was unknown not many years ago ; nevertheless, whilst these have become more liberalised, originality of character has been sacrificed by the artificial state of things which constitute the usages of society. Society, instead of conscience, has grown up to be the innermost governing principle of the people, and its mandates are powerful as those of law. So long as one meets the demands of society he is fitted for any position, but originality of character is seldom, if ever, cultivated by society. The mode of reasoning adopted is not as to whether a certain course of action to be taken be right or wrong, but whether worldly gain or loss will accrue therefrom. On the gain side is considered money, favour, distinction ; and on the loss side is considered the cost, whether it be unallowable, and under what penalties of law or society ; and on whichever side the considerations preponderate, that decides the course of action to be adopted, while the higher spiritual intelligence of the being, altogether separated from selfish considerations, is seldom appealed to for guidance. Whilst the tendency of the teaching of the Churches and society is thus to keep man enslaved under the lower animal instincts, animated by no higher promptings than those of selfish gain, kept in check by fear of punishment, science and education are declaring for the emancipation of mind, and the spirit of inquiry after truth which these are stimulating will bring man to a knowledge of a higher end in existence than that simply of material gain. All true advancement of the human race rests upon education and enlightenment, and the one essential of enlightenment is a desire for truth with originality of thought and freedom of expression. The use of education itself, however, is misconceived at the present time, for instead of being means to an end, usage has perverted it, as it were, into being an end to means : that is to say, instead of mind being cultivated to maturity in its natural growth to bear its greatest fruits for the use of all, it is stunted with unsuitable graftings in order to pander to individual fancy or worldly gain ; or, in other words, the popular ambition is to educate to a certain general standard, altogether independent of whether the faculties are under or above that standard—as to whether the languages or other subjects undertaken are likely to be of any practical use to the student through life, and without reference as to what the peculiarities of the mind or the physical condition of the student may be. Powerful natural faculties are possessed by many of those entering our universities, which, if cultivated with especial reference to their direction of force, would produce men of great genius in some particular line of life, but which, through misdirection of one phase and overstraining of another phase of character, have been ruined. Such minds would be better served with an elementary education in reading, writing, arithmetic, and geography, and a healthful occupation of body, which would afford inherent genius an opportunity of expanding by force of natural character. Although education is made so difficult in our best establishments as not unfrequently to dwarf the natural faculties in their growth, yet there are subjects upon which, in the interests of mankind generally, instruction should be given to all, but which, nevertheless, are very seldom undertaken. Every one, for instance, should be taught where the principal organs of the body are situated, and what their functions are. Melancthon remarks:—" It is shameful for man to rest in ignorance of the structure of his own body, especially when the knowledge of it mainly conduces to his welfare, and directs his application of his own powers." Each should be taught the leading chemical properties of articles of every-day consumption, and the distinctive effects of their use upon the body ; each should know the effects of inhaling good and bad air ; each should know how to float in the water or swim ; each should have healthful exercise to develop the physical system ; and each should be taught, in a word, to know and feel that the greatest duty he owes to his country and to himself. is

F

to cultivate a strong spine, as a good sound mind and body depend very much on that ; and with these, a cheerful countenance, cleanliness, a clear conscience and a happy and prosperous career generally follow, leaving behind a healthy and improving progeny.

Mrs. Ellis remarks that :—

"A cheerful temper—not occasionally, but habitually cheerful —is a quality which no wise man would be willing to dispense with in a wife. It is like a good fire in winter, diffusive and genial in its influence, and always approached with a confidence that it will comfort and do good. Attention to health is one great means of maintaining this excellence unimpaired, and attention to household affairs is another. The state of body which women call bilious is most inimical to habitual cheerfulness ; and that which girls call having nothing to do, but which I should call idleness, is equally so. I have always strongly recommended exercise as the first rule for preserving health ; but there is an exercise in domestic usefulness which, without superseding that in the open air, is highly beneficial to health of both mind and body, inasmuch as it adds to other benefits the happiest of all sensations, that of having rendered some assistance or done some good. Let me entreat my young readers, if they feel a tendency to causeless melancholy, if they are afflicted with cold feet and headache, but above all, with impatience and irritability, so that they can scarcely make a pleasant reply when spoken to—let me entreat them not simply to run into the kitchen and trifle with servants, but to set about doing something that will add to the general comfort of the family, and that will, at the same time, relieve some member of the family of a portion of daily toil. I fear it is a very unromantic conclusion to come to, but my firm conviction is, that half the miseries of young women, and half their ill tempers, might be avoided by habits of domestic activity."

Combe holds that :—

"The admirable harmony established by the Creator between the various constituent parts of the animal frame, renders it impossible to pay regard to or infringe the conditions required for the health of any one without all the rest participating in the benefit or injury. Thus, while cheerful exercise in the open air, and in the society of equals, is directly and eminently conducive to the well-being of the muscular system, the advantage does not stop there—the beneficent Creator having kindly so ordered it that the same exercise shall be scarcely less advantageous to the proper performance of the important function of respiration. Active exercise calls the lungs into play, favours their expansion, promotes the circulation of the blood through their substance, and leads to their complete and healthy development. The same end is greatly facilitated by that free and vigorous exercise of the voice which so uniformly accompanies and enlivens the sports of the young, and which doubles the benefits derived from them considered as exercise. The excitement of the social and moral feelings among children engaged in play is another powerful tonic, the influence of which on the general health ought not to be overlooked ; for the nervous influence is as indispensable to the right performance of respiration as it is to the action of the muscles or to the digestion of food."

" In order to form the minds of children, the first thing to be done," says Mrs. S. Wesley, "is *to conquer their will.* To inform the understanding is a work of time, and must proceed by slow degrees, as they are able to bear it ; but the subjecting the will must be done early, for it is a strong and rational foundation of a religious education." Mrs. Stowe says that "children will grow up substantially what they *are* by nature, and only that."

Tertullian, in speaking of the treatment of children, remarks :—" I esteem it better to keep children in awe by a sense of shame, and a condescension to their inclinations, than by fear." While Barnes remarks that :—

" Children should not be flattered, but they should be encouraged. They should not be so praised as to make them vain and proud, but they should be commended when they do well. The desire of praise should not be the principle from which they are taught to act, but they should feel that the approbation of parents is a desirable thing ; and when they act so as to deserve approbation, no injury is done them by their understanding it. He who always finds fault with a child, who is never satisfied with what he does, who scolds and frets and complains, let him do as he will, breaks his spirit, and soon destroys in the delicate texture of his soul all desire of doing well. The child, in despair, soon gives over every effort to please. He becomes sullen, morose, stupid, and indifferent to all the motives that can be presented to him, and becomes indifferent as to what he does, since all that he does meets with the same reception from the parent."

" A great part of the education of every child consists," says Professor Masson, " of those impressions, visual and other, which the senses of the little being are taking in busily, though unconsciously, amid the scenes of their first exercise ; and though all sorts of men are born in all sorts of places—poets in towns, and prosaic men amid fields and woody solitudes—yet, consistently with this, it is also true that much of the original capital on which all men trade intellectually through life consists of that mass of miscellaneous fact and imagery which they have acquired imperceptibly by the observations of their early years."

"Children generally," says Locke, "hate to be idle; all the care, then, is that their busy humour should be constantly employed in something of use to them."

Education, in its true sense, can only be a benefit when it is used to promote, assist, and develop nature. It should therefore be made more diversified and less irksome; and any natural force of character should be cultivated in its true direction. Get a phrenologist to examine your children's heads and tell you what their talents specially befit them for. Originality, both in youth and manhood, is too much tabooed, and copying or fashion is the order of the day. The prevailing idea is, that all knowledge is to be attained from the books of the learned, and all greatness by following the example of the great. Under this mad rushing pursuit after knowledge and example amidst the wilderness of books in their path, our best faculties are every day being done to death. No one can rise to true distinction by the mere copying of others, although a generally diversified study may tend to raise many to a good general standard. Many may attribute their success in life to the example of others, but for any one to lay down for his life-long example the rule of life adopted by another will never raise him head and shoulders above those around him. There are obvious reasons why this should be the case, and one of the most potent is, that no two minds are precisely similar in all their features, and that combination of faculties which would suit a certain course in life for one mind to bring it out in its greatest force, would not be at all suitable for another and entirely different combination of faculties. As minds are not all alike, so is it that different minds regard the same things from different points of view, and although such minds may arrive at the same conclusions, they do so very often upon different data. Some persons ridicule the idea, for instance, of the spirits of deceased acquaintances making their unseen presence known by means of raps and table movements, whilst others, who have attentively listened to pulpit-preaching for years without being able to realise the truth of an after-state, and in consequence became confirmed materialists, have been awakened into inquiry by those simple raps, and have afterwards obtained such evidence of the continued existence of their deceased friends as, to their minds, was conclusive. They have been led onward, if their desires have been pure and holy, from the receipt of answers to questions by this very slow and unsatisfactory means of communication to what might be considered the more rational evidences which mechanical writing have unfolded; and from thence onward to perhaps impressional or inspirational writing or speaking.

> " Not to understand a treasure's worth
> Till time has stol'n away the slightest good,
> Is cause of half the poverty we feel,
> And makes the world the wilderness it is."—*Cowper.*

There is no good but which, by perversion, does not lead to evil; and so with spiritual phenomena. A person who attains to mechanical writing should not return to table-rapping, and an impressional writer or speaker should not return to mechanical writing, and no mediumship should be abused, or used for trifling, selfish, or low purposes. The evils arising from circles for table movements consist in the loss and intermixture of individual magnetism, and they should not be habitually resorted to. The evil arising from sitting alone for mechanical writing consists in the disturbing influence which is brought to bear upon the nerve current; for the hands or arms are moved to write by means of an external current of magnetism applied by spiritual agency to the nerves of the arm and hand, and this current interrupts the natural nerve-current generated in and circulating through the body. Being too much resorted to, mechanical writing causes a depressing, painful weakness in the region of the heart, through the want of muscular force to give motion to the heart, and a loss of pulse is observable from this interference with the natural circulation of the blood. Nux vomica with nitrate of potash is found to give relief in such cases. The influence in sitting for impressional writing, on the other hand, is not of so disturbing a character, as the mode by which it is effected is supposed to be through the establishment of a magnetic current between an outside spiritual intelligence and the brain of the writer, so that the ordinary nerve-current dispersed from that quarter is not so much disturbed thereby. Impressional mediums may receive impressions almost at any time, so long as the mind is in a favourable condition; but they should never seek frivolous or selfish impressions, nor make an idle pastime or indulgence of this natural power, and they should never seek anything without first well considering whether they intend to use it, and, moreover, use it properly. Nothing short of personal experience can, however, educate the mind upon all the conditions necessary. The most important is, perhaps, never to regard the spirits of departed friends in any other light than that simply of friends. The universe was not created by spirits, nor is it spirits who clothe the lily of the field or teach the birds of the air how to build their nests. Man may sow and till, and spirits may influence and minister to the mind, but the Father alone it is who giveth the increase. Those whose desires are upon Him, in all fervour and purity, readily attract to themselves, unsolicited, all the assistance which their friends in the spirit world can afford, if their assistance be worth having; for, so to speak, all that are not with Him are against Him, and all that are for Him are of one mind and accord, and labour not for themselves, but that His will may be done. There are a great variety of "mediumships," or modes by which information may be conveyed from invisible spiritual intelligence through man. In some cases the mediums are conscious of the nature of these communications as they are being made through them, while in others they are not conscious of the nature of what they articulate or write. There are mechanical writing mediums, whose hands write at times in languages which they cannot themselves read; there are unconscious trance mediums, who speak things of which they have no knowledge, and there are inspirational speakers, who at times speak what they themselves have no knowledge of and cannot afterwards repeat or recollect—as the unlearned Apostles each spake in languages they knew not (Acts ii.). Cerebration meaning "the exercise or action of the brain," it may be said that while receiving these spiritual communications there is, in some cases, "conscious cerebration" on the part of the medium, while in other phases there is "unconscious cerebration" on the part of the medium. In order to understand this, it becomes necessary to know the distinction between the mind (spiritual animating intelligence or soul) which exercises the brain and the brain itself. The brain is simply the visible material nerve-machine of the spiritual animating intelligence or mind, and it conforms in capacity to its direction of exercise. As the body has a spiritual form as well as a material form, so has the brain a spiritual form ; but the animating intelligence is an innermost sublimate, residing with it by reason of their affinity. At will, this innermost intelligence, in the trance condition, may recede, and allow another intelligence to control the brain and the whole organism of its material body. In that state it is very slenderly connected (as by a very fine thread current to its material mansion), and it may or may not be conscious of the nature of the communication made through its material organism, although cerebration actually occurs, inasmuch as the brain is exercised, and through its instrumentality articulation occurs. Although memory is subject to the call of external circumstances, it is evident it resides almost altogether, if not altogether, in the invisible animating intelligence ; and if any such thing as " brain printing " takes place, the impressions must be of a very fleeting character to what they are on the immaterial mind. For impressional writing, on the other hand, although it becomes necessary to will the animating intelligence to remain passive in the writer, while another intelligence exercises his brain, in most cases he is conscious of the nature of the communication as it is made through his material organism, and he may remember it. There are, therefore, both " conscious " and " unconscious cerebration," noticeable in the several modes by which man may receive communications from invisible spiritual intelligences. In the class of influence previously referred to as that of electro-biology, where, by passes between two persons (the one in a positive frame of mind and the other in a negative), a magnetic current is established, through which, at the will of the positive mind, the material organism of the other person may be controlled, there is " conscious cerebration " taking place, but of a different character, inasmuch as the negative brain may be enslaved or become subservient, for the time being, to the will of the positive mind.

Having traversed the subject of mediumships superficially, and the bearing thereon of the theory of "unconscious cerebration," it becomes necessary to pursue the subject of "natural religion," by asking what is the most momentous question which any one can put to himself? What is the object of his present existence? It is all very well to consider the past, and especially the future, but they should only be used wherewith to improve and make the most of the present. The present duty is, no doubt, to make the best use of the mind and faculties, means and opportunities, that we enjoy. Reason guided by conscience, enlightened by an ever-striving after truth, doing all in love, to the best of our ability, towards all men. In his search after truth, such is the nature of man, that by a continuous desire for light, shaking off from his mind the errors imbibed from false teachings, and by placing himself in a condition to receive it, he may not only understand the real objects of his own existence, but he may also gain a wide knowledge of the things around him from outside intelligence.

Of course there are in nature many elements quite beyond the comprehension of man. There are also many elements which, by his own unaided senses, he could never find out and understand, yet which he may understand, if he will but apply his reasoning faculties to them when they are unfolded to him by intelligences freed from the grosser affairs of a worldly residence. At the same time, in his pursuit of knowledge he should remember that it is not because he is endowed with reasoning faculties of a certain capacity that he is therefore able to comprehend all those things which are within the ken of intelligences more enlightened than himself. Mind can only receive according to its capacity and without favour, for if there were any things hid from one that are not hid from another, it would be difficult to know which was right or which wrong; but where all things are open to all according to the capacity of mind to understand, it is quite clear there are no outside preferences. Some minds will of course reject the proposition that superior knowledge may be attracted by desire from unseen intelligences—for that which the mind cannot receive it necessarily rejects as impossible. So indeed are the laws of nature working, that all which is not in affinity gives place, as it were by a law resembling specific gravity, to all that which is in affinity; and in ratio to the force of affinity or attraction to each other do all things find their place. Place and condition, whilst being generally used to express different meanings, in such matters express much the same meaning, as nothing can reside out of its proper place, and its place expresses its condition relatively. It is evident from this that the common saying, "Order is Heaven's first law," expresses a great truth. It is, of course, impossible to say what is the precise nature of the causation of force in our material world or where it resides. The profound refinement of that department of nature in which it resides is altogether too great to admit of its exploration by our most refined and spiritualised minds. If light, heat, and electricity are equivalents of motion, and if motion is the equivalent of force, it might be held that force comes of the attraction of magnetism on the one hand, and of the repulsion of combustion on the other. The one great motive force of attraction to our material world might be ascribed to an invisible magnetic centre residing in the direction indicated by the magnetic needle, while the other, the great force of repulsion, might be ascribed to our sun, itself electrically ablaze from the combustion of magnetism radiating from the great magnetic centre. Be this theorising as it may, there is assuredly no want of harmony in the laws of nature. If there were, it would be regarded as a very Babel; for so complex are its ramifications, and so closely do they all depend upon each other, that the mere exercise of individual will or desire makes itself felt, so to speak, throughout the whole system in which it occurs.

Thomas of Malmesbury is credited with the following wise remark :—

"There is no action of man in this life which is not the beginning of so long a chain of consequences, as that no human providence is high enough to give us a prospect to the end."

Binney too expresses his views on this subject very forcibly thus :—

"A *right* act strikes a chord that extends through the whole universe, touches all moral intelligence, visits every world, vibrates along its whole extent, and conveys its vibrations to the very bosom of God ! Pray learn to understand how all work has in it a spiritual element ; how the meanest thing on earth has a divine side ; how all temporary forms include essences that are to be eternal."

Man's constant aim should be to study God's handiwork, to live in harmony with His laws in nature, and to make "self" subservient to His will in all things.

Much good might be done by the ministers of religion if they would earnestly stir church-goers up to a spirit of anxious inquiry after truth by appealing to their reason—if pulpits were constantly interchanged amongst the various persuasions—if doctrinal and sectarian teachings were avoided, and if the passing concerns of the day and the laws of nature were used to impress high spiritual truths and wholesome moral lessons upon the minds of hearers. Such a course need not interfere much with the churches of the day, while it would certainly tend to harmonise religion more with the example of Christ, and better entitle it to be called Christianity.

Bishop Porteus holds that :—

" Christianity forbids no necessary occupations, no reasonable indulgences, no innocent relaxations. It allows us to use the world, provided we do not abuse it. All it requires is, that our liberty degenerate not into licentiousness, our amusements into dissipation, our industry into incessant toil, our carefulness into extreme anxiety and endless solicitude."

Croly says that :—

" Christianity has no ceremonial. It has forms, for forms are essential to order ; but it disdains the folly of attempting to reinforce the religion of the heart by the antics of the mind."

Colton, with especial reference to the ancient superstitions and traditions, and the modern designs which have been grafted into Christianity, disfiguring the teachings of Christ, remarks :—

"It may be well said of many who would be displeased with you if you did not call them Christians, that had some of the ancient heathen sages lived to the present day to see their abominations and vices, they would have despised that faith which produced no better works. Alas ! how has the social spirit of Christianity been perverted by fools at one time, and by knaves and bigots at another; by the self-tormentors of the cell, and the all-tormentors of the conclave."

If truth be earnestly sought for, it will assuredly be found (John xiv.) : " If ye love me, keep my commandments : and I will pray the Father, and he shall give you another Comforter, . . . even the Spirit of truth, whom the world cannot receive, because it seeth him not, neither knoweth him." " The Comforter, which is the Holy Ghost ; he shall teach you all things " (ch. xv.). " The Comforter, even the Spirit of truth, which proceedeth from the Father, he shall testify of me " (ch. xvi.). " The Spirit of truth will guide you into all truth ; for he shall not speak of himself, but whatsoever he shall hear that shall he speak, and he will show you things to come." The conscience, or spiritual animating intelligence received through our brain, is identical with the Comforter, Holy Ghost, or Spirit of truth ; and if the commandments of Christ (love the Lord thy God, and thy neighbour) be kept, we shall soon, without seeing it, know and recognise the actuality of the presence of the Comforter; and if we seek his guidance, he will guide us in all truth, and show us things to come ; for he speaketh as he heareth from the Father, in whom there resides perfect wisdom and a knowledge of things to come.

It is a mistake to suppose that the Holy Ghost (Spirit of truth or conscience) was not to be present until after Christ's crucifixion. John the Baptist, it was said by the angel, should be " filled with the Holy Ghost from his mother's womb." Peter knew Christ because it was revealed to him, and Christ said that " No man can come to him except the Father draw him,"—that is to say, by the law of God in nature, the mind must be so enlightened by its experiences as to realise that true wisdom and lasting happiness can alone be attained by the animal nature being made subservient in all things to the spiritual or divine guidance of conscience or the Holy Ghost. Christ's mission on earth was to sow in the minds of men certain advanced spiritual truths. The minds of men were, by growth and experience, arriving at that stage to be able to receive those truths. From being guided, as heretofore, by low material instincts, acting in all things either under the inducement of reward or the fear of punishment, Christ desired that man should be led, by the purer and higher aspirations of his being, to act without selfishness or incentive in reward or punishment, and to be guided by his quickening spiritual animating intelligence or conscience. Christ having a purity of body (with mind reincarnated of a perfected spirit that had existed before "Adam," and upon whom, at about his thirtieth year, John witnessed a spirit or influx of magnetic fire in shape as of a dove descend), was chosen as "the light of the world." As he said, " I am the living bread." " I came down from heaven, not to do my own

will, but the will of Him that sent me." " If any man eat
of this bread, he shall live for ever, and the bread that I will
give is my flesh." " It is the spirit that quickeneth, the
flesh profiteth nothing, the words that I speak unto you,
they are spirit and they are life." Witnessing the ripening of mind around him, he exclaimed once :—

" Say not ye, There are yet four months and then cometh
harvest? Behold I say unto you, Lift up your eyes and look
on the fields, for they are white already to harvest (the minds
of the people were ripe to harvest). Believe me, the hour
cometh when ye shall neither in this mountain, nor yet at Jerusalem, worship the Father. The hour cometh, and now is, when
the true worshippers shall worship the Father in spirit and in
truth. God is a spirit and they that worship him must worship
him in spirit and in truth."—*John* iv.

Again, he likened his teachings to "a little leaven
which leaveneth the whole lump." In comforting his disciples before the crucifixion, he said he would not leave
them comfortless, but would come to them. " The word
which ye hear is not mine, but the Father's which sent me."
" These things have I spoken unto you being yet present
with you, but the Comforter, which is the Holy Ghost, whom
the Father will send in my name, he shall teach you all things,
and bring all things to your remembrance whatsoever I
have said unto you. Hereafter I will not talk much with
you." While he was with them, their spiritual wants were
fed by his pure inspirational teachings, but his mission
was to show the disciples, and through them all men, that
they might themselves receive through their own spiritual
animating intelligence (conscience or Holy Ghost) such
comfort and spiritual guidance as they required at any
time, either during his presence in the body with them or
after his crucifixion and departure. All things would be
brought to their remembrance after his crucifixion, either
during their then present lives, long after the ordinary
powers of recollection could be expected to serve them, such
as was realised in the extraordinary precision and concurrency
in which the writings of the history of his teachings as
furnished in the Gospels exhibits, or while in other bodies,
which they might afterwards exist upon this world in.
Although the disciples would have to be reincarnated in
other bodies and remain as " the salt of the earth " upon it,

until his second coming, and although in those other bodies they might forget what he had told them, as well as other things belonging to their pre-existence, yet their enlightenment of spirit would remain and be in them the Comforter, and through the Comforter or a pure conscience, by holy desire, they might attract revelation by which they should be taught " all things," and should be reminded of the pure spiritual teachings which Christ had also received of the Father, and had before taught to them. These teachings consisted of pure inspirational revelations of the laws of God in nature, by which man might better understand and fulfil his mission upon earth. One injunction which the disciples received was : " Let your light so shine before men that they may see your good works and glorify your Father." It must not be assumed that it is a matter of spiritual age altogether ; not so, for as Christ said, " Behold, those are last which shall be first, and those are first which shall be last "—for not every one that heareth shall receive. Those who, having had the same experiences and opportunities as the godly, and who continue nevertheless to resist the light, and refuse to have their wills made subservient to the divine will, shall be as the tares which were allowed to grow up amongst the wheat until the harvest. They shall be gathered before the wheat, and " consumed " by the tribulations which shall come in " the last days." Those days, we are told, " shall be shortened," that the children of obedience may be saved, and remain as shining perfected spirits, to inhabit the new earth that shall be prepared for them. The children of disobedience are represented as standing outside " the kingdom of heaven," with the door shut upon them, they weeping outside, while they would see the godly inside in a state of happiness. It must not be assumed that the godly will realise any happiness from the misery of others, for we are told there is more joy in heaven over one sinner that repenteth than over ninety-nine just persons. This figure must be taken, then, we suppose, to represent the remorse of conscience which will be experienced by the disobedient upon finding the opportunities of happiness which they have lost, and on becoming aware of the immensity of time that must necessarily elapse before another " Church " or harvest of perfected earth-spirits can be gathered, in which they may participate in the happiness of.   A public writer thus correctly describes a law in operation that is ever being exhibited :—

"Nothing raises the price of a blessing like its removal; whereas it was its continuance which should have taught us its value.   There are three requisitions to the proper enjoyment of earthly blessings :—a thankful reflection on the goodness of the Giver ; a deep sense of our unworthiness ; and a recollection of the uncertainty of long possessing them.   The first would make us grateful; the second, humble ; and the third, moderate."

It is obvious that a religion more suited to enlightened mind is now required—a purer Christianity—a religion of God and not of Mammon.   Man must eradicate from his mind the teachings of theology and fashion, and submit only to the guidance of a divine, untarnished conscience.   Some may say, " It is not to be done ; where is conscience ?   We cannot see it."   In reference to the blind way in which people refuse to acknowledge the existence of things simply because they cannot see and feel them—like Thomas the disciple, who insisted as a condition of belief that he must see in his hands the print of the nails, and put his finger into the print of the nails, and thrust his hand into his side— people who will neither look for evidence themselves nor examine into the correctness of evidence submitted by others —well was it remarked by the great teacher :—" The world cannot receive because it seeth him not."   Have they ever done a palpable wrong without being made aware of its presence ? Pain is not seen but felt, and so we know the sensation and admit its reality.   So with the Spirit of the Holy Ghost and truth.   We cannot see it, but we feel it ; there is no running away from it, and there is no escaping the conviction of its reality.   It is a balance in which every design and action of man is weighed, and if the Mammon side of the beam is relieved and cleansed from the corrosions and accumulations with which false teachings have weighted it, then will it be restored as the true guiding power and natural monitor of religion.   Where erroneous conceptions of spiritual obligations are implanted in the mind by false teachers, they falsify the lights of natural conscience, and the soul is pained and injured in those who adopt such false teachings every time they violate such erroneous convictions, just as much as if they violated the highest divine law, for it is the deliberate violation of a conscientious belief which tarnishes the mind or soul and makes the "sinner." Thoes who send the young out into the world with minds in which are inculcated a belief that certain actions are "sins" displeasing to God which are not really so, place as it were a millstone about the mind or soul, which sinks it into darkness and degradation. Teach, for instance, that man was made for the Sabbath, and not that "the Sabbath"—according to Jesus' more enlightened view—"was made for man," and instead of man exercising his mind to judge as to what is the best use to put it to in his particular case, whether it be open-air relief from a week of confined toil in order that his whole being may be refreshed and elevated, or whether it be church rest from a week of open-air exposure in order that he may grow in spirit while the body is resting, and you will sink man into the conscientious conviction that what is right on Saturday is wrong on Sunday, as if fixed laws and principles of right and wrong could be changed one day in every seven, from the moment the hand of the fallible household clock pointed to a certain figure, or we, by reason of every seventh rotation of the earth, were brought to face the sun. There is only one "sin" that cannot be pardoned, and that, said Jesus, is sin against the Holy Ghost. When man acts deliberately against his conscience he darkens it, and therefore the forgiveness of friend, foe, or priest is of no avail; and it is only through this dear-bought lesson of experience that man may benefit, by avoiding a repetition of the commission of the same error, so that his conscience may regain brightness by resisting the inclination to the same error the next time it is presented to him. Hence, nothing should be imposed upon conscience but what God in His wisdom places there. It might be well, in this view of the subject, if the general habit was dropped of making children conscientiously believe that certain trifling delinquencies, which at most are but personal offences—such as picking a flower or a strawberry, or tasting the sugar or jam—were serious sins in God's sight; for it is simply the imposing of "heavy burdens grievous to be borne," and such as Jesus charged those who sat in Moses' seat with teaching without themselves performing. Under teachings of this kind violations of conscience occur, whereas, if the minds of children were left natural, they would grow under the encouragement of a purity of conscience undefiled by human tradition and custom. Those who teach that such things are "sins" are "blind leaders of the blind" (Matt. xii.). "Jesus went on the Sabbath-day through the corn, and his disciples were an hungered, and began to pluck the ears of corn, and to eat." The Pharisees complained that they acted "unlawfully." Jesus asked them if they had not read that David and those with him had entered into the house of God and eaten of shewbread, of which it was only "lawful" for the priests to eat. Then turning round upon them, he said, "If ye had known what this meaneth, I will have mercy and not sacrifice, ye would not have condemned the guiltless." It is God's earth, air, and sun under which the corn and flowers and fruits grow. God alone it is that gives the principle of increase or growth. Properly speaking, all things are God's; and instead of man claiming ownership, at most he can but claim stewardship. The more closely the laws of nature are investigated, the more apparent becomes the uniformity of their operation in their various departments; hence the conclusion that matter in its various forms is but the clothing, or outward and visible sign or expression, of the condition of an inward progressive invisible intelligence. The law of progression in material existences, each having its appropriate span, beginning with its birth, reaching maturity, and then declining with its decay and death, was referred to in the early part of this work. The researches of geologists show that the earth itself has been inhabited from time to time by more advanced forms of life, and this demonstrates the ever-fitness of things, and the correctness of the conclusion that matter, as matter, is after all only a changing visible sign. Two elements are concerned in material things— namely, the visible and invisible. As the body and mind of man fitly represent what has been attracted to them, so does this earth itself fitly represent the condition of its inhabitants. There is a certain invariable intimacy between mind and matter, by which they grow hand in hand, and are always in affinity or in consonance with each other, each expressing the condition of the other. The very principle of progression or growth, both in mind and matter, is alike or uniform in its operation, and the history of all the several existences through which the invisible intelligence in man has passed, is exemplified in the history of the material of which the body of a man is composed. To make this understood, it is necessary to re-state that all force and life is produced by the magnetic affinity which characterises all elements in nature, whether in earth, air, water, or their inhabitants. Two elements drawing together by reason of their affinity or magnetic attraction for each other, cause a vital growing invisible force which, according to their power of affinity, the distance they are separated, and other conditions, varies in power and expression or sensation. The closer they approach each other not only is their speed towards contact accelerated by momentum, but it is also increased by the increasing power of the attraction exerted by each drawing more closely to the other, and when the heat generated by such increasing velocity reaches a point which the elements thus being drawn together cannot withstand, combustion and repulsion are the consequence. The conditions of matter, therefore, conform to the force with which it is propelled, and any elements which may be in combination with bodies thus travelling towards each other, whose velocity is thus accelerated, which may fail to continue to accurately represent the growth of mind in the mass of the bodies which is expressed by the velocity attained must necessarily be subjected to more intense heat than they can withstand, and thus, by combustion and repulsion, they are relieved from contact—and, suffering disintegration, are at liberty to seek new affinities or form new combinations. Powell uttered a great truth, although rather obscurely, when he remarked, "God is now spoiling us of what would otherwise have spoiled us. When God makes the world too hot for His people to hold, they will let it go." The grain of wheat contains two elements in magnetic affinity, and only requires contact with earth, and the generation of the properties of decay and combustion, in order to allow them to work together to produce electricity and a new combination or growth, which, in turn, attracts by magnetic affinity with the all-pervading intelligence, that intelligence suited to its organisation or wants, and propagates its own kind—its own invisible intelligence passing onward at death, and being attracted by force of its aspirations or wants towards other more advanced states of

G

existence. All things have intelligence suited to their requirements, from the rocks—whose particles know how to combine invariably in what chemists term " definite proportions," and know how to disintegrate themselves invariably under certain other conditions—to vegetable and animal life, through their various stages of birth, maturity, and death in each existence—where growth, motion, digestion, and propagation are noticeable. In some cases an intelligence is exhibited by some of the lower orders of the so-called " animal kingdom," such as the ant and zoophyte, through their nervous systems merely (they having no brain), which is astonishing to contemplate ; and this illustrates the correctness of the conclusion, that all things in nature receive intelligence according to the requirements of their organisations and wants, whether expressed through the brain, or direct through their nervous systems or otherwise—for no sooner are the two elements in magnetic affinity acting in unison in that mechanical law of nature by which a vital electrical force and growth is originated, than another higher law of nature is brought into operation, by which the necessary intelligence is drawn to supply the requirements of the new material form, which is to visibly express that intelligence. Where vital force is generated, followed by growth, it is sustained and progresses by a beautiful compensating law, in its own use or exercise causing a want or compensatory attractive force. As the arm of man is made strong by exercise, so the mere operation of vital force increases the strength of structure by attracting fresh elements for more vital force—and, as vital force increases, therefore, in its operation, it attracts additional intelligence from unseen nature on the one hand, and additional matter on the other hand from material nature, suited to its growing requirements, and to visibly express the quality of its mind. As with matter so with mind. Man's spiritual nature has wants represented in the higher aspirations of his mind—and the exercise of these wants attracts to him the necessary spiritual sustenance. The operation of this law has been fully realised by all who have used true prayer, by exercising fervent, pure, spiritual desire—and its citation here is that of a well-established known law of God in nature, and not mere speculation or theory. The influence gained by the exercise of this phase of our being is of the nature of treasure laid up in heaven, where neither moth nor rust doth corrupt, nor do thieves break through and steal. It is that which, by seeking for, we shall find ; which, by asking for, we shall receive ; and which, by knocking for, will be opened to us. It is that which Jesus alluded to at the well, when asked by his disciples as to whether he would partake of food, when he said, " I have meat to eat that ye know not of." On that memorable occasion it was he said (John iv.), " Woman, believe me, the hour cometh, when ye shall neither in this mountain, nor yet at Jerusalem, worship the Father. . . . The hour cometh, and now is, when the true worshippers shall worship the Father in spirit and in truth : for the Father seeketh such to worship him. God is a Spirit ; and they that worship him must worship him in spirit and in truth." There is a great equalising tendency at work throughout all departments of nature. And we can scarcely imagine how a high angel can descend to perform a grand mission of love and goodness to us money-grubbing people, experiencing, as he must do, a painfully chilling sensation, making him very anxious to get away from our corrupting influence as soon as possible, without that angel knew that his goodly action was like the planting of seed which would soon grow and produce much fruit. Such was the influence experienced by Jesus, no doubt, after mixing with and scattering his lofty truths amongst the multitudes, for he felt the exhausting effect, and hence he had so frequently to isolate himself for prayer. He was wont to withdraw himself to high mountains apart, where he might breathe in a purer magnetic atmosphere, be freed from disturbing influences, and be nourished and strengthened in spirit by such supplies as his nature and his mission required or wanted. The action of a pure and highly spiritual mind like that of Jesus in prayer is like the action of a lightning conductor. It establishes and draws down a current of pure magnetism, by means of which the higher conceptions of truth may be impressed— and, the light thus received, through pure minds, is like the little leaven that leaveneth the whole lump, for, not only does the one impressed benefit, but the purer magnetism thus drawn circulates through others, and their minds, in turn, yearn for advancement, and also draw light. That earnest desire which is now so generally evinced for truth, will, no doubt, by this same law, attract an increased enlightenment of mind, more ennobling conceptions of God, and wiser and purer incentives in matters of every day life—a practised and not simply a professed Christianity. This mode of reasoning once established, there will be infinitely more ground for anxiety at the hitherto prevailing indolent custom of accepting, without investigation, teachings which violate our reason when fairly submitted to it, than there will be for anxiety at that craving for truth which now investigates and now rejects what the mind cannot understand.   The question raised by scientists as to whether life is the result of certain invariable mechanical laws in nature, has startled some who have rushed to the conclusion that an attempt is being made to propagate atheistical opinions, forgetting that the very acknowledgment of the existence of such laws implies an All-wise lawgiver, their author and executor.   Regarded in the light in which it has here been placed, it will be seen that the generation of vital force, by a mechanical law in nature, results only from the method by which the Divine mind governs matter through the properties given to it.   Instead, therefore, of matter governing force, or originating mind, what is observed is simply a process by which the Divine mind is made manifest to us through the Divine laws governing matter.   Mind is the only source of all-enduring power—the Divine mind having, in omnipotent wisdom, organised the laws which beget vital force in matter.   All things are fed with intelligence or mind by attracting or drawing it according to their requirements or stage of growth ; hence no power can be wielded by any creature of God in the material world so great as that which can be exercised by a man of enlightened mind, who, acting in harmony with nature and in obedience to the laws of God, draws his inspiration from Him.   Jesus once said :—

" The words that I speak unto you, I speak not of myself, but the Father that dwelleth in me He doeth the works. . . . He that believeth on me, the works that I do shall he do also ; and greater works than these shall he do ; because I go unto my Father. And whatsoever ye shall ask in my name, that will I do, that the Father may be glorified."

The power which may thus be wielded by the exercise of

the human mind is far beyond anything which people will now credit. If matter is regarded as a symbol or expression of mind, sensation may be regarded as a type of intellectual growth, for the lower we descend in the order of creation, the lower are the types of sensation discovered. The ox, for instance, is not so sensitive to pain or to pleasure as man, and some men are not so sensitive to pain or pleasure as others. The senses, too, act as the educators of minds, enabling them to recognise, more or less uniformly, certain properties or conditions in matter for the purposes of intercourse, and the more advanced the intellect, the greater the powers of sensation, and the larger the stores of knowledge it may draw from its surroundings; hence, the senses of an intellectual mind will enable it to discern agencies which will inevitably lead to certain effects, whilst the dull mind, with inferior powers of sensation, unable to perceive those agencies, has no evidence of their existence, and will even cavil with the other as to the truthfulness of their respective convictions. There are certain minds which, by reason of their advanced perceptions, are cut off from general intercourse, as it were, and become estranged to those amongst whom they live. These are sometimes called " men in advance of their time," and their opinions living after them, are afterwards approached by others who come to recognise in them their sublime worth, and these same minds are then frequently beloved, and they are referred to by the next generation, perhaps, as those sages who lived and died. When men come to recognise that revelation is ever open to them—and when, in all purity of mind, they suffer themselves, in the will of the Father, to be led by impression, they will discover that they are led by a higher intelligence than that represented by the deductions of their own reason, because of the very limited data or powers of observation which their material senses can possibly compass. The senses were given for use, but when the mind has been enlightened to discern that it may draw greater power and wisdom by communion with unseen intelligence possessing powers of observation vastly superior to its own, its ordinary reasoning powers should induce it to seek such guidance, especially in matters of spiritual concern. Referring to the senses, and the laws which govern their action, the following, taken from an

Australian paper, may be read with interest and advantage :—

"Our minds have been so long accustomed to look upon things which come within the range of the bodily senses as the only realities, that the man who regards them in a truer light, and who is bold enough to acknowledge and to live up to that truer light, is deemed a madman or a fanatic. Yet, when we consider the proofs of the existence of those things which are seen, and compare them with those of the reality of the unseen and intangible, we cannot fail to be struck with this most patent fact, that the visible things are unreal, while invisible things are the true realities.

"In nature, the mind is led gently up to the comprehension of the unseen by a series of steps to which the five senses give the clue. Of these, touch is the simplest, and the lowest in the scale of being ; no animal, however elementary, being destitute of it. By touch we know, or we think we know, of the presence of objects which are in contact with us. By taste we know certain qualities of those objects which are beyond the reach of simple touch, qualities whose existence we would deny if human beings were possessed only of simple nerves of touch. By smell, we feel assured of the existence of vapours, gases, and fine dust of solid substances, which are beyond the grasp of the two lower senses ; which are, in fact, unrealities to those who can only touch and taste. In all these three modes of acquiring knowledge of things around us, actual contact of these objects is essential. Unless they touch us, or penetrate within the mouth or nostrils, and mingle with their moisture, we are ignorant of their existence. We have been led from solid and fluid objects merely to the understanding that there are finer and more ethereal existences than these, but still pressing close upon us, and around us. The fourth sense, hearing, leads us first into the realm of the intangible. We become aware that objects, more or less distant from us, have an existence, because we *hear* them. Nothing material passes between; no tangible messenger arrives to touch our ear ; only the soft air lies in the interval—as it always does even when no sound is heard—and yet we know that the thing which gives the sound exists, and even are aware nearly in what direction it lies, and how far away from us. How is this ? Are we not already overstepping the limits of gross perception and giving credence to the immaterial ? The messenger called Sound is certainly not a material existence in the ordinary acceptation of the word ; and if one man only in the world possessed the sense of hearing, while the rest could only feel, taste, and smell, he would be regarded as a wild enthusiast and visionary, a dabbler in an unknown world, whose life, being guided by this added sense, would be esteemed madness and delusion.

" But what a world is opened up to him who is blessed with sight, the fifth, the last bestowed, and the most wonderful, of all the senses ! To hear a sound, the air is absolutely necessary as a mediator, as a material road upon which the immaterial messenger may travel ; for if we ring a bell within the exhausted receiver of an air-pump, no sound is heard. But the sense of sight requires no such material road for its myriads of messengers to use, as they bear their bright despatches to us from distant objects, far beyond the reach of sound. Looking through the glass receiver when it is full of air, we see all that is placed upon the other side of it ; and when the air is all pumped out, and the blows upon the bell within it are quite inaudible, we not only see as clearly as before, but may prove by tests sufficiently delicate that an actual *obstruction* to the passage of the rays of light has been removed. That immaterial messenger, called Light, not only does not require a material road, as in the case of sound, but travels best when all material things are swept away. The rays of light from stars, at distances from us absolutely inconceivable, fly with a speed equally inconceivable in a straight line through the interstellar spaces for thousands of years, and meet with no hindrance or impediment until they enter our atmosphere, and pass through the lenses of our eyes or telescopes. Light, therefore, that intangible messenger from distant suns and systems, needs not even the lightest natural material to convey it, but in every portion of the universe finds it only an obstruction to its progress.

" Thus, without passing the range of our own senses, and the familiar round of objects presented to our minds through them, we are confronted with a problem which involves the acknowledgment either of an insoluble mystery, or of the existence of two things, motion, and a medium for its transmission ; neither of which, by any ordinary definition, can be termed material portions of the world of Nature.

" For light is motion ; nothing more. And the medium, the thing moved, no man has ever detected by the most delicate experiment. It is not only beyond the range of every human sense,—although all space, and even our very bodies, are filled with it,—but it is beyond the power of detection by the most cunning apparatus ever yet devised to aid our senses. How, then, can we feel assured of its existence ? By a very simple process, to which, with our usual verbosity and pomp of words, we have given the fine name, Reasoning by Analogy. If we drop a stone into a pool, a quiet pool, of water, a little circular wave rises round the stone as it sinks, and gradually spreads, circling outwards, until it breaks upon the shores. But, as we repeat the experiment, and watch little floating objects upon the surface, we find that it is not the *water* which is displaced and projected outwards, and which travels onwards, but only the *wave*.

The surface remains in the same position as regards the shore, while the wave, the upraised circular ridge, or ripple, speeds outwards and onwards to break upon the shore, carrying, as it were, the intelligence of the blow given to the water by the stone. Now, what we observe to take place on a small scale in the quiet little pool, may be seen upon the widest ocean, on the occasion of a submarine explosion, or earthquake shock. A tidal wave. as it is termed, spreads outwards in all directions, and in a few hours encompasses the globe, overwhelming low-lying shores, and carrying destruction into ports and harbours—and bearing also to these shores the news of the submarine upheaval of the waters caused by the outburst of the earth's interior fire. This news-bearing wave travels at a speed of hundreds of miles per hour, while the greatest speed of rushing water does not amount to more than a small fraction of that velocity. Again, we become aware that it is not the water which travels onwards, but the wave which travels through the water. But what is the *wave* as distinguished from the *water*, its vehicle of propagation? Once more we must admit an existence which is not material, since a wave of this kind is simply Motion. When a rifle ball is fired, the motion resides in the ball, and takes its vehicle, its material envelopment, along with it. But here we have Motion, an immaterial thing, passing *through* water, yet unaccompanied by water, or by any material garment whatsoever.

"Now, what is seen to occur in bodies of water may be also demonstrated to have existence in the atmosphere. The atmosphere is simply an ocean, of lighter, finer, and more elastic material than the sea, encircling the globe, and submerging in its blue profundities all the dwellers upon earth, and even the highest mountains. The barometer serves as a plummet to sound its depth in every portion of the world, weighing, as it does, the column of air which stands above it, and deducing from that weight its height. We cannot ascend to the surface of the atmospheric sea to view the vast billows which roll upon it ; but we know of their passage, and of the lines in which they travel, by the barometric soundings which are taken every few hours in every habitable portion of the earth. There is no mystery in this ; it is precisely analogous to the behaviour of the fish in ocean depths, who know, by the pressure of the water upon their internal air-bags, precisely what height of water stands above them. We have means to ascertain that atmospheric waves are upon the pattern of ocean tidal waves, and are indicative of Motion of a special kind, speeding onwards overhead, not *accompanied* by air, but *passing through* it.

"So far we have dealt with surface waves upon both sea and air. But there are waves which do not appear upon their surface, and to us these are at the present most important, since they come within the range of a lower sense than that of sight.

"Along the banks of certain quiet rivers in Africa, and in other portions of the world, are tribes of natives, who, guided by Divine impression, make use of a very simple kind of telegraph. When a native wishes to communicate with a friend at some distance, he chooses a time when his correspondent is likely to be bathing, diving, or snaring wild fowl in the river ; and, entering into his own portion of the river with two large pebbles, he knocks them together sharply under water in a cadence pre-arranged. The blows are distinctly heard at a distance of a mile or two by his friend, if his ears are under water ; and the signals are replied to in a similar manner. Now, here the surface-ripple, produced by the knocking of the stones together, speedily dies away into the river banks ; this, which has already been described, is, in fact, what is termed a ' wave of elevation.' But the shock and vibration of the stones below the surface sets in motion what is called a ' wave of compression,' rapidly spreading outwards in a circular form, and depending on the elasticity of the water, or its slight compressibility for its action. This wave of compression is propagated very rapidly from atom to atom of the water, and proceeds very swiftly down the river, from the native who gives the signal to him who receives it. As the wave surges against the drum of the ear of the listening native, he understands that it represents the clink of the stones in the hands of his friend. The action of this wave is very simple. Suppose we suspend a number of marbles along a rod, so that they shall nearly touch each other as they hang freely in a long row. Now, if we give the marble at one end a tap with another marble in the direction of the rest, it will tap against its neighbour, which in its turn will tap the next, and that will pass on the blow to the next ; and thus the whole line of marbles will in succession receive, and pass on the blow, immediately falling back into its place again. The marble at the far extremity of the line will fly outwards to some little distance, and show plainly to the eye that the motion had been transmitted through the marbles, and had remained in the last one for a time. This is a very simple experiment, but it involves a most important fact. The motion given to the first ball *resided in it,* and carried its body with it as far as it would go, but, when it was stopped by the second ball, the animating force left its temporary dwelling-place, and passed onwards to the second ball, carrying it forward until obstructed by a third ball. Here, although the second ball is stopped, the invisible, intangible, impalpable, and immaterial force which animates it, leaves its second dwelling-place, and becomes, as it were, embodied or incarnate in the third—and so on to the end of the series of marbles, which represent its successive embodiments or incarnations. This seems to afford, at the very outset, food for our mental digestion, as showing that force, or mind —for these terms may be shown to be convertible—has an indestructible existence apart from body, apart from that visible, tangible, and ponderable shadow, which we denominate ' matter.'

" As with the marbles so with the watery atoms clashed in succession against each other, and this contact is passed onwards with amazing speed, until the last particle is dashed against the ear of the listener placed under water, making him aware that the two stones at a distance have been struck together. In other words, he hears the sound of them, and this is the way in which fish hear the sound of objects dropping into the water. In this way also motion travels *through*, not *with*, the water.

" But an essential element—as we may see by the experiment of the suspended row of marbles—in the ready transmission of a wave of compression, or a sound-wave, through a series of particles of fluid, solid, or gas, is that there shall be a certain distance between these particles. If they were close together no wave could be transmitted in this manner through them, since there could be no *compression*. Air and gases are peculiarly suited to the transmission of waves of compression, because their particles are more widely separated than those of fluids and solids ; in other words, they are more elastic and compressible.

" It will be readily seen that wherever elasticity and compressibility exist—and they exist in a greater or less degree in all things that we know—waves of compression may be transmitted. But, as a medium of transmission of such waves, the atmosphere stands first of all, and indispensable. Every movement that we make sets up a series of waves of this kind, radiating in every direction outwards. When these movements are sharp and sudden, the waves they originate break upon the ear as sound. When they are sharp and frequent, as from the beating or vibration of the vocal chords of the throat, they fall upon the ear as a prolonged rattle, roar, or note, just as they are less or more rapid in pulsation. All musical notes are thus produced, and are nothing else than more or less rapid successions of sound-waves.

" When the explosion of a large quantity of gunpowder took place on the Thames near Erith, a few years ago, the quantity being much larger than in the late Regent's Park explosion, three circular waves of compression started at the same moment ; one through the water damaging the shipping, another through the earth, travelling to great distances where the stratification of the rock was favourable, and another through the air producing the effect of concussion, or sound. So great was the impetus of the atmospheric wave, that, at about twenty miles' distance, the Crystal Palace at Sydenham rocked to its very base and appeared about to fall, and large plate-glass windows in London were driven into fragments, while the sound appeared as if close at hand. So violent was the river-wave that seamen were flung from the decks of vessels at more than a mile's distance. And so powerful was the earth-wave, starting from the same centre of explosion as the two other waves, and similarly circling outwards, that the steeple of an old church at Bedford, one hundred miles distant, was irretrievably damaged by the shock of this artificial earthquake. We find that these three materials transmitted, each after its own fashion and in its own time, a great wave of motion to distances which seem almost incredible, and at a speed so vast that we must estimate the time occupied, even in travelling to Bedford, only by seconds. Now let us ask ourselves, *What* went to Bedford? Not the air, because it could not travel at a hundredth part of that speed, even in a hurricane. Not the water of the Thames. And still more absurd it would be to suppose the solid earth capable of moving to such a distance from its natural position. Then what travelled there? We do not know a word by which to call it. No man has ever seen it, felt it, or weighed it, and yet its effects are most palpable and evident to our senses. It can travel through earth, air, and water, and exhibit itself in motion, perhaps destruction, everywhere for miles around ; but is itself invisible, intangible ; —is it, therefore, unreal? Can the effects be real, and the cause unreal? No sane mind will reason thus, but must admit a real Cause when its effects are manifest. We cannot here escape the admission of the reality of the Unseen, and of the unreality in comparison with it of those things which are seen. A consideration of the phenomena of light and heat proves beyond a doubt that a still more subtle ocean exists, which is indispensable to the transmission of waves of light and heat, as air is indispensable to the transmission of those of sound. The behaviour, also, of light waves is identical,—as proved by the phenomena of reflection, refraction, and diffraction,—with that of air-waves, and waves of water. So that, although we cannot by any human sense perceive,—even by the most delicate apparatus added,—this omnipresent ocean, we know that it possesses tenacity, elasticity, and a certain density ; and that it is a real existence. But it cannot be set down in the category of material things, since it is imponderable, intangible, invisible : and yet it is the only means by which we see, by which we are warmed and lighted, clothed, housed, and fed !"

The principles propounded by materialists seem very plausible at first sight to thinkers, but when they are carefully investigated they are found to be altogether without basis and finality. They build upon the assumption that "matter governs force," while, in fact, it might as well be held that "force governs matter ;" for, in the order of nature, they are as dependent upon each other as are the nerve-current and force which works the heart and the blood circulation for preserving health in the human body. Materialists may assert, if they will, that to matter pertains the property of motion by reason of the affinity or attraction of particles. That property of matter is, however, designed by mind, for it is a principle upon which all harmony in nature is preserved; and it would be as reasonable for any one looking upon extensive machinery in harmonious action to assert that "material governed the force" in the machinery, instead of acknowledging that the steam, being confined within the iron, was only a part of the argument, while the heat and water and iron had all to be brought together by the design of mind before the steam could be generated, or before the boiler and machinery could be fashioned to hold it and utilise it. To mind is due the property of force which is obtained in steam from heat and water; and to mind is due the property of force which is obtained from the material iron in which the steam force is governed; and to mind is due the design and governing of the machinery. It cannot be fairly said that scientists hold any such materialistic views. On the contrary, they acknowledge evidences of mind superior to material. That "motion develops life" is the next tenet of the materialist's doctrine; but they ignore at this point the attractive or affinity property of matter in the generation of life. The scientist, on the other hand, is willing to affirm a belief that by a mechanical law of nature vital force is generated; and in this conclusion he sees grounds for a more profound and reverential admiration of the infinite wisdom of God than under the old theory of special action of a personal God. The materialist then goes another step forward by holding that "life develops thought;" and, consequently, that "life and thought are only modes of that motion, which is an inherent quality of eternal matter." The scientist here confronts him by asking "How matter became endowed with such qualities— qualities evincing such profound wisdom, the mere possession of which exhibits design and authorship of infinite mind? The materialist does not believe in mind existing after death, or before properties were given to matter. He will admit that matter is indestructible, and that by a law of nature nothing can be annihilated or wasted;

nevertheless, he holds the belief that mind perishes at death, and that it has no hereafter. The logician here steps in and says to the materialist : " If, as you hold, matter is eternal, and has ever been endowed with the power of developing mind, and that matter is indestructible —how then can mind perish ? " The materialist thus appears to be a man who has gained a little knowledge, and then become too stubborn to receive any more. If he would exercise fervent spiritual desire he would, no doubt, realise the existence of an all-wise, all-pervading, invisible intelligence, by which he may gain a knowledge of things unseen which will convince him. Happily the " salvation " of the human race does not require that people should either depend upon the investigations of scientists or the teachings of sectarian ministers. Each one must investigate and seek for light in the spirit of truth to obtain convincing evidence within himself upon which to hang his faith. The Father has left open an avenue of communication to man, in revelation, by which the pure in mind may always draw from the source of all truth untarnished to satisfy his requirements. Such was the character of the knowledge in the youthful unlettered Jesus, by which he astonished the doctors in the Temple, and with which his spiritual teachings, as recorded in parts, abound ; and such was the wisdom which inspired the apostles after the Crucifixion, and under which they spake in several languages they had not been versed in. By revelation, then, evidences of truth reach man altogether independent of book learning. Man does not comprehend all the laws and influences which govern matter and life. His reasonings and deductions can only, therefore, be based upon some of the conditions through which results are brought about, and they are, therefore, constantly proved erroneous ; and thus he cannot tell what is going to happen in the future except by inference. The materialist, however, cannot disprove that revelation and prophecy have gone thus far, for " things to come " have been revealed, altogether independent of human reasoning and deduction. Hugh Miller says :—

" The footprint of the savage traced in the sand is sufficient to attest the presence of man to the atheist who will not recognise God, whose hand is impressed upon the entire universe."

"An atheist," remarks Jeremy Collier, "if you take his word for it, is a very despicable mortal. Let us describe him by his tenet, and copy him a little from his own original. He is, then, no better than a heap of organised dust, a stalking machine, a speaking head without a soul in it. His thoughts are bound by the laws of motion, his actions are all prescribed. He has no more liberty than the current of a stream or the blast of a tempest ; and where there is no choice there can be no merit."

When man learns by experience that "all is vanity" in the material sense, when he is brought to realise that true happiness can only be attained by a strict obedience to untarnished conscience, and when his every desire is that not his own but the Father's will may be done, and he learns to live for others and not for self, the visible Church will be replaced by the spiritual Church as foretold in Jeremiah xxxi. 33, 34. At the present time the angels of God are preparing for the ingathering of the new Church, and if people would follow the teachings of God in His unerring Book of Nature they would realise in their simplicity, truthfulness, and beauty, a better sense of how they should live. Those invincible principles by which such perfect harmony is sustained, and all things are kept moving with such wonderful precision within their respective orbits, unfold to the mind of any one who studies them a perfect lesson of life. Take, for instance, that property of affinity which all elements have for each other, and we have the leading lesson confirmed as to loving each other. Consider, then, the law of the attraction of affinity which is always being exerted by all elements upon all other elements in nature which surround them outside from themselves, and we learn that it is designed that all our exertions should be directed altogether in unselfishness towards others outside of ourselves or our own immediate circle. Ponder, then, carefully over that law by which a union of elements in affinity generates vital force,—those elements having been attracted to each other under the unselfish conditions which have just been stated,—that union, by vital force, attracting in turn intelligence suited to the new organisation, and you will recognise in that law a lesson of most inestimable value to the human race, showing, as it does most plainly, what are the natural and most godly conditions under which union or marriage should take place, and the necessity, in the interests of mankind, that exists, why man's progeny should have the most perfect, healthful, natural, and harmonious organisation, in order that it should thus be fitted for the enshrinement of the purest and highest condition of mind and godlike spirit.   Pearls are not cast before swine, and if the organisation is not of a high character, how may it be used as an instrument for the expression of the higher phases of intelligence?   When the mind dwells upon the condition of things around us, and yearns to discover a new code of laws and customs under which men may dwell in greater harmony with each other, and through which ignorance, strife, vice, poverty, war, and disease may be overcome, let it contemplate those laws by which worlds travel through space millions of miles to complete their orbits to a fraction of a second.   There is no jarring there, and these are "for signs" unto those who would study their ways for lessons of daily life.

Hugh Miller remarks :—

"Nature will be reported : all things are engaged in writing its history.   The planet, the pebble, goes attended by its shadow.   The rolling rock leaves its scratches on the mountain, the river its channels in the soil, the animal its bones in the stratum, the fern and leaf their modest epitaph in the coal.   The fallen drop makes its sculpture in the sand or stone ; not a footstep in the snow, or along the ground, but prints in characters more or less lasting a map of its march.   Every act of man inscribes itself in the memories of his fellows, and in his own face.   The air is full of sounds, the sky of tokens, the ground of memoranda and signatures ; and every object is covered over with hints which speak to the intelligent."

Man, however, in his greatest knowledge, can scarcely reach an approximate idea even of the vastness, the magnitude, or the grandeur of Almighty God's infinite universe. Take light, for instance, travelling at 77,000 leagues per second,—such is the distance of the Polar Star, that light from it takes 50 years to reach our Earth—or, in other words, if it were to be eclipsed or "annihilated" we should continue to receive its light for 50 years after the occurrence.   From stars of 6th magnitude, light takes 1042 years to reach us, while from stars of 14th magnitude it takes 100,000 years to reach us.   Figua, in his "After Death," remarks :—"As naturalists now aver that man has existed on the Earth only within 100,000 years, some of the stars now seen may have been extinct at about that time !"

The Milky Way's length is about 800 times the distance of Sirius to the Sun,—a distance which is 1,373,000 times greater than that from the Earth to the Sun. Herschel, examining from the Cape of Good Hope, estimated the Milky Way to contain 18,000,000 of suns ; and so great the distance between, that light from a star at one extreme would take 15,000 years to travel, and light from that star would be received on Earth about 8000 years after it left.

"Our Sun appears to advance with the whole system in the direction of Hercules at the rate of 62,000,000 leagues per year, or two leagues per second, describing an orbit of millions of centuries. There are worlds lighted by two, three, and four suns—white, blue, red, green, and yellow."

The great god-principle and secret of good government, which is specially noticeable throughout all nature, is that the greatest harmony and happiness for each and all can only be secured when the exertions of the individual members are altogether directed in unselfishness for the benefit of all others, and when the wisdom and power of those exertions are drawn in humble fervency from Almighty God, the source of all knowledge and strength. Yet, if the customs of society, its habits and thoughts, and its legislative enactments, are referred to in order to see how far these leading principles of nature are applied to matters of every-day life, what do we discover ? Why, the desirability of using such legitimate means as are at his disposal for the improvement of the physical and mental calibre of his race is a subject which receives little or no attention from man. He will toil a lifetime to gather a little money, which must be left behind, and, perhaps, to the lasting injury of his children ; but, to look out a woman for a wife in mental affinity and suitable physical condition with himself, thus to gain future happiness, and to leave behind him better people, never occurs to him—his selection being based entirely upon selfish motives. Thus, a wealthy consumptive man will marry a poor but healthy woman—or, a rich woman, inheriting disease of mind, will marry a healthy poor man of good mind—and neither will think of the absolute wrong done in handing down the "sins" of the parents from generation to generation in that way. There is no law prohibiting such marriages, and it is not the custom of society or of religionists to frown upon

them. A diseased pair, or one inheriting mental derange-
ment, have only to fee a parson, and this "watchman on
the wall" will only be too happy to join them in what he
calls "the holy bonds of matrimony"! There is a vast
divergence noticeable between the courses indicated by godly
unselfish procedure and that of worldly self-gratification in
such matters. If such people doubt their own value before
marriage as progenitors, they have only to apply to an
assurance company for life policies, and, from the " medical
man's report," &c., they will soon discover, by putting
" self " in that way to the test of " self," how their life
value, when it becomes a matter of money-making, in the
estimation of others is depreciated through their faulty condition. While touching upon this subject, it is not enough
that the selection should be good, for the results depend much
upon the general conduct of couples—and if virtuous living
is necessary in single life, it is more so in the married state.
What the world wants is " fewer and better children ; " and
it would be well if legislation could be adopted to direct a
better tendency in such matters. There are sanatary laws,
and vaccination is made compulsory by Act of Parliament,
but there is no legislation to prevent, under penalty, the
propagation of criminals, idiots, and people of diseased
minds and bodies, born under the cohabitation of unsuitable
and unhealthy people and drunkards ; and, until that is
provided for, the tendency of vaccination, it is held, must
be prejudicial to the more healthy children inoculated, if
the matter be from unhealthy children or those inheriting
disease. As a matter of Political Economy, it is of paramount importance that the causes of mental and physical
degeneracy in communities under civilised and progressive
forms of government should be well explored, and amendment made. By legislation punishment is meted out to
criminals,—the public health is cared for, and contagion is
guarded against by compulsatory inoculation,—and gaols,
hospitals, and asylums, are provided to alleviate society
from its crime, its sick, its poor, its lunatics, and its drunkards. Advancing legislation is beginning to discover that,
to properly administer to such evils, it is necessary to cope
with the causation, and so effectually remove them at their
inception rather than to nurse them at their maturity. It
is found, for instance, that as ignorance and extreme poverty

H

are the first conditions of " sin " and " crime," the cheapest and most effectual way of dealing with these is to withdraw state grants-in-aid from churches, and devote the money towards making education compulsory, free, and secular,— as has been done in Victoria,—and to afford the poor every facility for their improvement otherwise. While large streams of emigration are pouring out people from old centres to populate new countries, intermarriage, climatic change, pure air, and healthful occupations, tend greatly, it may be supposed, to promote the general physical stamina of people—and, as emigration ceases, and large populations become centred, it may also be supposed that their physical condition will suffer. Advancing scientific discovery will probably meet this threatened degeneracy with improved sanatary and other provisions ; and if legislation keeps pace with the necessities of the people, there will be effec-tual legal means adopted to protect society against the evil consequences of unhealthy propagation by the castration of all children physically unsuitable for improving the race. For, it is obvious that as the owner of cattle improves his stock by using only the choicest of kinds, and weeding out of all inferior sorts, so is it of paramount importance, when the improvement of our own species is concerned, to adopt exactly the same course. If such a course was faithfully carried out, what vast benefits might be reaped by man-kind from this work even in a single generation, for with the excision of physical degeneracy, it must be remembered that crime and a host of evils would be greatly reduced, and, indeed, mankind would fairly be regenerated in the spiritual as well as in the material sense. Selfishness, ignorance, and prejudice, are the only obstacles to such reform. As, however, reforms are mostly gradual, and we are here to do the most good practicable, we may hope that the time is not far distant when legislation will make provision for the issue of marriage licences by a competent Government medical officer, certifying as to whether the species is likely to be improved or not by the marriage of intending couples, and the parents of every unhealthy child not born under wedlock, or under such medical licences, might very reasonably be subjected to a penalty. In any case, it is high time that the selfish custom under which people propagate children in ignorance, under unfavourable and wrong conditions, should be guarded against by the State by the printing of an outline of conduct, to be handed to all male and female aspirants, to whom medical certificates might be granted; and no marriage should be consummated by registrars or ministers of religion until solemn affirmations be made by male and female that they have carefully read over such printed outline of conduct, and fully understand its meaning, and will adhere as closely as they can to the advice tendered. That false delicacy which prevents a mother from explaining to her daughter, and a father to his son, the duties of the married state before they enter upon it, should be discarded. As well might agricultural skill and good crops be expected from a novice in farming, or good stock be reared by one who had no knowledge of the conditions and kinds necessary to insure successful breeding. If the man own a superior mare or cow, he will take care to observe certain natural laws which are considered inevitable in their operation when he selects mates for them, in order to improve his stock, and he will take care not to allow them mates if their health or condition is being impaired by too rapid propagation, or by other causes. If the agriculturist wishes to grow crops, he too will look well to the conditions of the soil, and the seed, and the science of cultivation required by natural laws, and will not exhaust his farm by injudicious or over-cropping. If the same laws were observed by men towards some of their poor wives, whose health and strength are being pulled down by bearing children too rapidly, it would save many a valuable mother that can ill be spared as the guardian angel of her children, and greatly reduce that hoard of puny degeneracy which every year is raised, to the deterioration of mankind. The laws of God in nature are inevitable. Young people should consider well the ascertained laws of nature by which the character and nature of the parents are transmitted to their children. They should remember that as they sow, so may they expect to reap; and what person, having sown tares, can expect to reap wheat? It is one of the highest and grandest duties that can be discharged by man, and it is one of the chief teachings sought to be inculcated by the philosophy of "natural religion," to awaken mankind to the necessity of using every means which knowledge can reveal for the improvement of its own species. People should be wisely paired, both with a view to physical and mental improvement in their offspring. If man or woman, through faulty physical or mental condition, be not calculated to bring healthy and wise children into the world, they can commit no greater "sin" than to marry and beget children. There should be a perfect harmony in thought and feeling between man and wife. The woman's mind should be relatively negative to that of her husband. Neither should impose hardship upon the other. The conditions surrounding their union should be pure and godly, and the secret purposes of the mind in both should be of an ennobling, pure, and philanthropic character; and there should be no bad, irritating, or low influences surrounding the mother during pregnancy. Mothers-in-law should be avoided, for it is harder for a wife to please husband and mother than it is for a man to obey two masters. It would be well if the laws of affinity in mind were better known and more acted upon in marriage. Men will send to the ends of the world for a superior kind of horse, sheep or dog, shrub or tree. If breed is worth so much care, and the knowledge of how best to improve and cultivate the structure of the lower animals, shrubs, and trees has grown into an important science, surely it is worth the attention of those who after death, if not sooner, will have revealed to them the fruits of their earth-life with pain or joy, and who owe a duty to their God and their fellow-man in posterity, to see their own race improved in like manner, both in body and mind. If people suffered themselves to be guided by an All-wise Divine Will, men and women of suitable mental and physical condition would be brought together, and the paramount importance of harmonious and pure parental thought upon their progeny, before and after birth, would, more happily for themselves and others, be realised. Beauty, position, and wealth, grafted in ignorance to unsuitable conditions, and led on under mere animal desires, propagate mental and physical degeneracy; whereas those in natural affinity, whose minds are made subservient to the Divine Will, fulfil one of the highest functions of their being, by bearing into the world those incomparably good and unblighted fruits—purity of mind and body. There can be no greater mistake than to imagine that the gratification of sensual desires lessens the intensity of such desires. The very reverse is the case, for the appetites grow stronger under cultivation or indulgence :—

> " Fie on sinful fantasy !
> Fie on lust and luxury !
> Lust is but a bloody fire,
> Kindled with unchaste desire,
> Fed in heart ; whose flames aspire,
> As thoughts do blow them, higher and higher."
> —*Fairies' Song, in*
> *Shakespeare's " Merry Wives of Windsor."*

It is suicidal ignorance, leading to the very worst of results, to shirk the requirements of natural law in such matters ; and were people fully aware that as every secret thought records itself upon the mind, and goes to make or mar it, and that of posterity, and that the consequences of every action performed during life will stand up clearly before the mind's eye in the after-state, as the fruit of our bodily existence, to bring joy if good, or sorrow if bad, to us, they would be able better to realise their obvious duty in such matters. With a view to make the after-consequences of our thoughts as well as actions more clear, if possible, it may be repeated that every evil thought mars the mind ; and as mind is our only stock-in-trade after death, we must necessarily awaken there with feelings of keenest sorrow when we behold the miserable stock which we have left to us to begin another existence with. "Lay up for yourselves," therefore, "treasure in heaven." Every thought or action is like a good or bad seed sown, and in the tree which it grows into, with its own characteristic fruit, there will stand a living monument to confront our eyesight after death. Our spiritual eyes, which are far more observant than the material eyes, will look with horror and sore regret and remorse upon all the miserable perversions of nature which have originated through us, while we will rejoice with untold happiness at the resplendent beauty which characterises all things that grow in harmony with God's laws. Such are the rewards of which "natural religion" teaches.

John S. Mill, on "Liberty," page 189, observes :—

" It still remains unrecognised that to bring a child into existence without a fair prospect of being able not only to provide food for its body but instruction and training for its mind, is a moral crime both against the unfortunate offspring and against society; and that if the parent does not fulfil this obligation, the State ought to see it fulfilled at the charge as far as possible of the parent."

To a certain extent, this proposition may hold good, for it may be admitted that the offspring of beggars generally follow in the footsteps of their parents, so that poverty, from this point, is perpetuated from mere parental influence. But all poor people are not beggars, and, apart from beggars being made from parental influence, a great many beggars are being constantly made by the objectionable modes of aiding the poor, which, as Southey observed, " were bad, for they took from independence its proper pride, from mendicity its salutary shame." Where is the utility of growing thistles in our garden, and of industriously striving to keep them from shedding their seed in season, when it is far easier and better to grow in their place pleasant flowers or useful trees ? As a question of " political liberty " the unequal division of property appears to be the great causation of poverty and ignorance. It is the duty of those who govern to see that one man has as good a chance as another to earn a living for himself and family ; and it is further the duty of those who govern, in the absence of equality in opportunities, to see that proper provision be made for the education of the children of those who are too poor to pay for it ; but, alas ! those who govern are mostly " born with silver spoons in their mouths," or they are under the influence of such, consequently they make laws to conserve their own selfish interests, to the neglect of the poor and their offspring. Some leading minds in our own day have been brought into existence under the conditions suggested by Mr. Mill,—and even Jesus was a child of the manger. Can it be said that those who brought such people into existence were guilty of moral crime ? If parents are in affinity—are in proper physical and mental condition—and are guided by pure and conscientious motives, the offspring, whether of rich or poor, are not likely to be a burden on society. With reference to the more equal distribution of wealth, there is a great God-principle in nature represented by the giving of all out to others according to their WANTS.

It may be asked, How far do law and custom adopt this rule of life and insure a fair division of the necessaries of life to all people according to their requirements? Do not land and mines belong to God, and were they not intended, as the rain and the sunshine, as much for the poor as for the rich? It may be held that once land is alienated from the Crown it would be unfair to the holders, and disastrous to established rights and interests, to disturb or question the titles. There are, however, occasions where legislative enactments disturb vested interests—and law will not recognise titles—and it is yet to be impartially tested as to whether much of the public estate has not fallen into hands that have given the public "no just or reasonable equivalent," and whether it should not yet, upon that score alone, revert to the public estate. In the colonies, where there are large tracts not yet alienated, it is worth serious consideration whether the ownership should not remain in the Governments, and their public revenues be chiefly drawn from their land-rents. What great harmony in society can there be looked for or reached, when monopoly is ever aimed at, and where the rich are becoming richer, while the poor are becoming poorer, and this state of affairs is brought about by the selfish tendencies of the laws? In England, for instance, where the legal ownership of the territory is claimed by a handful of people, and the immense wealth of the nation is collected in the coffers of a fraction of the population, while an immense number are in absolute want and wretchedness, the law of primogeniture is still perpetuated to the ruination and disgrace of the country. As was well remarked some time ago in a speech of one of her leading men :—

"The production of wealth is marvellous, but its distribution is not satisfactory. The relations between employers and their men are not so intimate or satisfactory as they should be. Remove the poor starved Tipperary labourer to a new country and he becomes a pioneer. How do you estimate the weal of a country but by the happiness of the great majority of the people, and not by the wealth of any class."

God is bountiful. Nature's stores contain enough for all and to spare. It is the selfishness and the avarice of man in trying to collect a plethora in his own possession in order that others may experience and be inconvenienced by a corresponding scarcity that brings suffering. By this means the few rich exercise a power over the numerous poor. This state of affairs represents an unwarrantable interference with natural laws, and it occasions, as all such interferences must inevitably do, mischief and misery. Dryden remarked that :

"Had coveteous men, as the fable goes of Briareus, each one hundred hands, they would employ all of them in grasping and gathering, but none in giving or laying out. Nature teaches otherwise, for all the parts of the universe, as they borrow of one another, so they still pay back, and that by so just and well-balanced an equality, that their payments always keep pace with their receipts."

Seneca wisely observed that :

"We are at best but stewards of what we falsely call our own ; yet avarice is so insatiable, that it is not in the power of liberality to content it."

"The lust of avarice," says Pliny, "has so totally seized upon mankind, that their wealth seems rather to possess them, than they possess their wealth."

"The avarice of the miser," says Colton, "is the grand sepulchre of all his other passions, as they successively decay ; but, unlike other tombs, it is enlarged by repletion and strengthened by age."

The amount of labour which suffices under ordinary circumstances to produce for man the necessaries of life, so far from being oppressive, is not more than sufficient to provide healthful exercise for him. By the interference with natural law, which the cravings of man for exclusive ownership and power represents, a large majority of people are denied the right to so much as occupy or use any portion of God's earth without paying other men " for the privilege," and their hours of labour are made burthensome beyond their physical requirements, and therefore lead to degeneracy ; while the affluent, in their ignorance of the consequences to themselves which are thus brought about, suffer the penalties of disturbed natural law, by growing physically and mentally weak, effeminate, degenerate, sickly, and miserable by luxuriant living and a want of healthful exercise, or a fair sharing in that over-labour which they impose upon their poorer brethren. Some employers are inclined to regard it as unfair for their hands to demand an increase of wage, forgetting to consider that if those hands find their hours of labour injurious or oppressive, or if the cost of their food, fuel, and rents are increased, they are as much necessitated to demand an increased rate of wage as is the manufacturer necessitated to increase the selling price of his goods when he is charged more for the raw material which he manufactures, the labour which he employs, or the money he requires to use. Flesh and blood should surely be as free as merchandise. It is said the poorer classes are wasteful. If this is applied to them, what can be said of the extravagance and luxurious indulgences of the wealthy, and the waste represented in their costly mode of living? Union is the only source of power left to the poorer classes to exercise, in furtherance of the rights of labour. "Lock-outs" and "strikes" may sometimes prove too costly for labourers to persevere with until their demands are attained, for it is not always that right can successfully compete with might at the onset. But if these "lock-outs" are costly to labourers, they are costly also to employers, and the loss sustained in this way on both sides will lead both parties to devising and establishing, in their mutual interests, systems of arbitration by which the rights of both may be represented and equitably weighed, and adjustments arrived at which hitherto have not been possible, so that, taken in this light, "strikes," if costly, may not be altogether profitless to labourers. The selfishness of the wealthy up to this time has been exerted to keep the bulk of their fellow-creatures poor and un-educated ; and the apostles of the wealthy will be found, even now, to lecture these poor people on the duty they owe to their country in such phrases as this, employed by a recent writer of some distinction :—" Political power lies naturally with Intellect and Property, and what God has joined man cannot put asunder with impunity." It is generally admitted that people should first be educated before they are allowed to exercise the franchise, and as an intelligent community is more orderly and easier governed than an ignorant one, it is obviously the first duty of those who wield political power to see that ample national provision is made for the education of the masses. The wealthy classes, representing much political power at the present time, however, understand perfectly well that a wider representation must necessarily follow general education, and that fairer representation means fairer government. Hence, the money interests of the wealthy classes tend to keep the people ignorant, that the poor may continue to do their work for them, make their money for them, fight their battles for them, and pay an undue proportion of the cost of those battles and of the general expenses of government. The world has arrived at that stage, however, that secular education must be made general, free, and compulsory in all enlightened countries; and the interests of the poor will demand and receive greater attention in other directions,—and, although the poor will, when educated, undoubtedly have increased representation, and the burthens of taxation will necessarily be thrown more upon the richer classes, it does not follow that the mental calibre of legislative representation will be in any way inferior to what it has been, for the electors will take good care to get the best men to represent them. When the education of the masses becomes general amongst nations, truly democratic or representative forms of government must follow, and the principles of government will be extended beyond present limits; and instead of the present wasteful cost of monarchies, with immense standing armies vying with each other for extent, we shall probably see that kind of thing reformed, and an International Code, with an International Court supported by an International Force, may possibly be organised to deal with all differences between nations, and to preserve peace between them. To return to the proposition of the writer just quoted, it is a fallacy to assume that the greatest intellect of England is centred, as a rule, in the propertied classes. In fact there is evidence opposed to this, for, under the law of primogeniture, there is great room for believing that the eldest boy who inherits the whole of the property is more likely to be inferior in mental capacity to his younger poor brethren, for, says a recent writer :—

"In first-born children the cranial bones of the fœtus are subjected to pressure which acts injuriously upon the cerebral structure. The emotional life of a primiparous mother is at the highest strain during the period of gestation. The prospect of untold suffering and new unexperienced joy gives to her mental attitude and entire nervous system an erethistic condition, and imparts this to her offspring."

The laws of Moses made provision for this period. Deut. xxiv. 5 : " When a man taketh a new wife . . . . he shall be free at home one year, and shall cheer up his wife." Speaking of the influences on the first-born, Dr. Langdon Down remarks :—

"These things exercise a marked influence in determining the ratio of idiotcy among first-born children, and males having larger heads than females meet with a more perilous egress."

Because a small section of the population represent the wealth, and, therefore, monopolise the power, are we to be told, then, that such a state of things is the most desirable for the general good, or at all consistent with the will of God as observed in the laws of nature? Whichever way we turn in nature, we find the law of compensation exercising an equalising tendency,—man may injure his fellow-creatures, but he cannot alter nature's laws. Whenever man does an action not in harmony with the Divine laws, that action, mischievous in itself, will inevitably produce other mischief; and thus mischief, like good, grows until, through the abhorrence generated by experience of its loathsomeness, it is removed. Are we to be told, then, when we observe evil consequences, that they are from "natural causes," or, in other words, that they are the best results which natural laws enable man to realise? Is the running ulcer to be cured by being covered over and hid from sight with sticking-plaster? Are squalid poverty, physical degeneracy, disease, absence of honest energy, and idiotcy, to be cured by the munificent manner in which the wealthy support poorhouses, hospitals, gaols, and asylums? The centralisation of great possessions and wealth in the hands of a few people, as already indicated, is opposed to observed natural laws, for these are found to be equalising and without discrimination in their systems of distribution. Thus, light and heat, and air and rain, come alike, and the earth yields her crops alike to good or inferior, rich or poor. This departure from the higher law of bounteous love—this centralisation and monopoly—consequently leads to inferior good or evil. In its season, such an order of things has, no doubt, served a useful purpose to some at the expense of others by administering to people in a form of mind unable to realise a necessity for a better and more ennobling condition—in ignorance they slaved and starved, and in their sufferings, through the darkness in which their minds were kept, they did not recognise that their hardships were imposed by their fellow men, and, therefore, not seeing the cause and not knowing any means of redress, they very often might be led to charge God with inflicting pains which in reality were inflicted by their fellow creatures. The eager craving for wealth and power has led to competition ; and, although this has had its concomitant good by leading to many important reforms and to general advancement, yet it has abused the public mind, for its secret impulse has been personal gain and self-enrichment; and this, bad in itself by its pernicious influence on personal mind, has borne its bad fruit by leading to untold frauds and wrongs. When the laws governing the action of the mind are better understood, and people can realise the injurious effects upon mind that are produced by exercising it with plans and intentions with a view altogether to obtain personal advantages over others, it may then be expected that general reforms and advancement, as well as individual spiritual progression, will be far better attained by a substituted exercise of pure, unselfish, inward thoughts and desires for the general good. Mind, as the inner temple of the living God, should be kept sacred, "clean garnished and swept." Some day, people will realise that it is impossible for the mind to be employed in schemes to obtain advantages over others, without, to the same extent, perverting it by the violation of one of the highest lessons of the spiritual life, which is that of unselfish love and the doing the best we can for others. [Luke xxii. : " He that is greatest amongst you, let him be as the younger ; and he that is chief as he that doth serve."] "What is a man advantaged," exclaimed Jesus very truly, " if he gain the whole world and lose himself?" "Whosoever exalteth himself shall be abased, and he that humbleth himself shall be exalted." "When thou makest a feast call the poor, the maimed, the lame, the blind, and thou shalt be blessed, for they cannot recompense thee." If the tendency of exercising the mind under selfish influences at the expense of others, is injurious to it, then it would be well to apply this knowledge to such minor concerns as have a tendency to injure the minds of young people. To this end, it might be advantageous to so alter or modify the rules of some

popular games and amusements, which are otherwise beneficial and improving, so as to do away with the prevailing
ingredient in them of selfish competition.   Referring to the
general prospects of Great Britain, judged of by the natural
course of certain known causes producing certain known
effects, notwithstanding that immense wealth has been accumulated by her people during the past few years, there
can be very little doubt but that her politicians will, ere
long, be confronted with difficult national problems, upon
the wise solution of which her future stability must depend.
Her manufacturing, commercial, and emigration interests,
for instance, will require close attention.   The large stream
of surplus population which has flowed outwards from her,
has not only tended to keep within limits the number of
mouths and producers at home, but it has opened up and
settled new colonies beyond the seas which have kept
largely and profitably employed the manufactories and
commerce of the mother-country.   As these colonies advance they acquire their own ships and their own manufactories, and although this may lead to greater prosperity
with increased employment in the colonies, it is a loss to
England, although undoubtedly it produces a certain compensating benefit by attracting additional immigration
from the mother-country by helping to drain it of hands
whose labour is no longer required at home for the manufacture of those articles which, through such a change, are
no longer necessary for such foreign markets.   By this
process, however, England loses her skilled artisans—while
her commerce is affected also—so that she loses by this
process the profits arising from the production of raw
material, the profits arising from the manufacture of those
materials, and the profits arising from the shipping carriage
of the commodities both in their raw and manufactured
conditions.   There are, undoubtedly, other extensive lands
which the Anglo-Saxon is destined yet to be implanted
upon,—such as parts of South America, Africa, Asia, and
New Guinea,—but the time cannot be remote when the
present large streams of emigration from Great Britain will
receive a severe check—and that will take place at the
same time that the colonies will have established their own
factories, will have their own skill and labour, will neither
require raw nor manufactured goods to any extent from

the mother-country, and will lose in her a market for their raw produce.   What will Great Britain do then with her surplus population, and her commerce, it may be asked, as she will then have no scope for their employment on her home or on foreign trade.   This is an aspect she should be prepared to face, for the settlement of new countries and all other progressive changes are brought about with extra-ordinary rapidity in these times.   Witness, for instance, the settlement and progress changes which have taken place in America and Australia within so short a time as the thirty years last past.   Of the people of Great Britain as well as of the rest of Christendom—people who profess to live under the teachings of Christ, yet who have per-verted these, and are living for the most part in a condition of fashionable listless indifference of mind, as mere pro-fessors of truth and not earnest searchers after it.   It may be said as in Rev. iii. :—

"I know thy works, that thou hast a name that thou livest, and art dead.   Be watchful, and strengthen the things which remain, that are ready to die : for I have not found thy works perfect before God. Remember therefore how thou hast received and heard, and hold fast, and repent. If therefore thou shalt not watch, I will come on thee as a thief, and thou shalt not know what hour I will come upon thee.   Thou hast a few names . . . which have not defiled their garments ; and they shall walk with me in white : for they are worthy.   He that overcometh, the same shall be clothed in white raiment ; and I will not blot out his name out of the book of life, but I will confess his name be-fore my Father, and before His angels."

The great changes indicated as likely to arise at no dis-tant period will not be confined to the mother-country, but will most probably be shared in by the whole world more or less ; and these changes may lead in some quarters to a state of great social demoralisation such as that indicated as marking "the beginning of the end" of the present era of existence upon this earth in Daniel xii. :—

"Shut up the words, and seal the book, even to the time of the end : many shall run to and fro, and knowledge shall be in-creased. . . . Many shall be purified, and made white, and tried ; but the wicked shall do wickedly : and none of the wicked shall understand. . . . And from the time that the daily sacrifice shall be taken away, and the abomination that maketh desolate set up."   Mark iv. : "Unto you it is given to know the mystery of the kingdom of God : but unto them that are without, all these things are done in parables." Mark xiv. : " And the gospel must first be published among all nations."

" But when ye shall see the abomination of desolation spoken of by Daniel," said Jesus, " standing where it ought not (let him that readeth understand) then, let them that be in Judea flee to the mountains." . . . " Except that the Lord had shortened those days no flesh should be saved." . . . " And then shall He send His angels, and shall gather together His elect from the four winds, from the uttermost parts of the earth to the uttermost part of heaven." . . . (The ingathering or new Church of ripened minds.) . . . " But of that day knoweth no man, no, not the angels which are in heaven, neither the Son, but the Father."

For those who attach importance to " Revelation," the following passages may be taken to allude to the light which is now being shed upon earth-minds, revealing to them the higher meanings to be obtained from scriptural teachings, till now held obscure under the seals of the Churches. Churchmen and laymen alike are now awakened, and are becoming anxious to know the higher truths contained in Scripture and natural laws, and this desire is drawing revelation to earth-minds through Christ, who, in spirit, is now opening the book, or, in other words, is throwing off the errors and fanciful figures of human invention under which his teachings have been locked up and obscured, and he is thus revealing the higher truths of God, as taught by him while on earth, to the enrapturing delight of those who receive these revelations. The passages from 5th chapter of Revelation are as follow :—

" I saw in the right hand of Him that sat on the throne a book written within and on the backside, sealed with seven seals. And I saw a strong angel proclaiming with a loud voice, Who is worthy to open the book and to loose the seals thereof ? And no man in heaven, nor in the earth . . . was able to open the book." . . . (The word of God as at present misunderstood and erroneously expounded by the Churches.) " And I wept much, because no man was found worthy. . . . And one of the elders saith unto me, Weep not : behold, the Lion of the tribe of Juda, the Root of David, hath prevailed to open the book, and to loose the seals thereof. And I beheld, and, lo, in the midst of the throne and of the four beasts, and in the midst of the elders, stood a Lamb as it had been slain, having seven horns and seven eyes, which are the seven Spirits of God sent forth into all the earth.

And he came and took the book out of the right hand of Him that sat upon the throne. And when he had taken the book, the four beasts, and four and twenty elders fell down before the Lamb, having every one of them harps, and golden vials full of odours, which are the prayers of saints. And they sung a new song, saying, Thou art worthy to take the book, and.to open the seals thereof : for thou wast slain, and hast redeemed us to God by thy blood out of every kindred, and tongue, and nation, and kingdom."

The fall of " Babylon " predicted in 18th chapter of Revelation might be held to apply to England.

" The merchants of the earth shall weep and mourn over her ; for no man buyeth her merchandise any more. . . . And the fruits that thy soul lusted after are departed from thee, and all things which were dainty and goodly are departed from thee, and thou shalt find them no more at all. . . . And every ship-master, and all the company in ships, and sailors, and as many as trade by sea, stood afar off, and cried."

Many other passages, having a similar bearing, might be quoted ; but, when inspiration is breathed through minds dwarfed by mythological and other religious traditional sophistries, its value is almost abrogated by the obscure language in which it is presented to us. The matters to which these passages refer, as well as the remarks referring to England and the world generally, must be received, therefore, as mere conjecture, and must be weighed by each one according to the light that is in him. They are taken to relate to the future, and it suffices people to know that if, in the present, they live in harmony with God's laws in nature—loving their neighbours—they need have no fear of the future, as there is ample evidence to show that God's creatures are cared for in a manner which as far exceeds the love of an earthly parent for his own children as pole is distant from pole. The law in nature, by which this wonderful care is exercised, seems to have been well known to Jesus, for, in order to exemplify its existence to the minds of his hearers, on one occasion, with great force of meaning, he exclaimed, " Are not five sparrows sold for two farthings, and not one of them is forgotten before God." " If the weal of countries," as an authority previously quoted very wisely remarks, " is to be estimated by the happiness of the great majority of their people ;" and if their happiness may be extended by the elevation, through education and political representation, of the masses, so is it with religion. Religions, like languages, represent the condition of intelligence of the people; and there is nothing which attaches such disgrace to the people of these times more than the fact that their religion is behind their scientific researches, behind their knowledge of natural law, behind the scope of their legislative enactments, and behind their fashionable, social, and moral restraints even; and that; while in all other concerns of life, they suffer themselves to be guided by the exercise of reason and reflection; yet, through indifference to their eternal happiness, by not searching out truth for themselves, they blindly accept the preaching of doctrines which will stand no such test. You cannot compass the technicalities of the arts and sciences in conversation with the wild aboriginal of Australia in his own language, for his intellect has not been cultivated to that point, and he has no language to express them in. In the language of the parable of the sower it is unreasonable to expect that seed which falls on the way-side, or on the barren rock, or amongst thorns and thistles, can come to anything; for it is either trodden down, eaten up by the birds, perishes for want of soil, or is choked; but from good seed sown in suitable soil, there is hope of an abundant harvest. So will it ever be with minds and religions. The advanced minds of the present time have outgrown belief in the religions of the Churches, and they require a faith which will bear the most crucial test which the knowledge they have gained of the laws of nature can apply. The greater the knowledge gained of the operations of nature the higher become the conceptions of Deity; and it is not too much to say that most cultivated intellects have learned enough from nature to convince them that the personal God of the Old Testament—who is represented as repenting, being angry and jealous, and as expressly directing the most wicked actions, and interfering with His own established laws—is not the character of that God which they see evidences of in nature—is not the character of that God who sendeth His rain and sunshine alike to the good and wicked, but that it is the faulty ideal God of darkened intellect, and the character there represented is utterly inadequate to express the all-wise and pure attri-

I

butes which are now entertained as residing in Deity. The more simple the form of religion, will generally be found the most pure. It is when man fashions his God after the pattern of man that complications, errors, and difficulties are set up, which can alone be corrected after man has gained sufficient knowledge of himself and of the laws of nature to see clearly that his pattern is as faulty, if not more so, as that of the worshipper of a wood or stone god of his own carving. Religion to be in the highest degree beneficial must be natural, and to be natural it must appeal to the understanding, so as to elevate the daily life, according to the intellect and spiritual requirements of the people. " Cast not your pearls before swine." A religion or a language that might suit a nation a thousand years ago, may not suit their descendants to-day. All religions have probably done service in their way and day. " Natural religion " aims at a cultivation of the intellect, and a constant investigation of the laws of God in nature, and an application of the principles observed in these laws to matters of everyday life, to elevate our conceptions of Deity, to promote purity of thought, and to bring about the true brotherhood of mankind by improving the customs of society and the tendency of legislation. It is not based upon supernatural evidences, nor upon dogmatic assertion, nor upon so-called miracles, but upon the never-varying established laws of an Allwise God. And this religion indicates to minds of ordinary intelligence what these laws are, and how they operate, under which man may commune with his Maker, and draw from Him all that is necessary for his requirements. It clearly defines the laws governing religion, and shows how they operate. It not only indicates the continued existence of the mind after death, aiming thereby to improve the life that is with the hope of a better one, but it shows the process by which each one, desiring evidence upon this point, may obtain it for himself. It not only indicates the existence of rewards and punishments, and a judgment whereby all will meet with their deserts, but it makes plain to powers of ordinary comprehension the operations of those laws which govern the thoughts and desires of the mind, whereby every exertion of these is self-registering, self-judging, and self-rewarding ; and it points out a rule of life under which all may make the most of both worlds. It not only acknowledges an Allwise, everywhere present God-mind in nature, and that God reveals Himself, but it sets Him alone up as the only infallible true guide of our being; and, while it acknowledges that we may learn and profit much from the revelations handed down to us through Scripture and otherwise, it bids us remember that revelation is ever open to all those who desire it, and that we must judge all things by the "Spirit of Truth," according to the light that we may so receive through it. It tells us to treat with charitable feelings the religious opinions of all men—yet admonishes each one diligently to search for truth in all things from the Father of all wisdom; and as the heavenly bodies not only receive light but reflect it out to others, so it tells us to let our light shine, in season, among men. Language avails little to convey the spirit of truth, which cannot be forced from one to another, nor purchased. It must be experienced, and be felt within each, "if ye will receive it." Hence it is that men are led astray by accepting as truth, without discrimination, all that is presented to them as "Divine Revelation," whether in the actual words of Scripture, or the definitions given of those words by their religious teachers. "Out of the fulness of the heart the mouth speaketh"—so is it with the language which is used by some men in their public expositions on spiritual sayings, the true meaning of which they have no real knowledge. It is very easy for any one to explain away difficulties to his own satisfaction, but if "self" enters into the consideration at all, the result will obviously be in sympathy with "self," and therefore antagonistic to the spirit of truth, whose whole desire is, "not my will, but thine be done." If in a disagreement between two persons upon any given subject, one seeks to adjust matters from his own purely selfish point, while the other is perfectly disinterested—which will receive the most? Surely it will be him who desired most; but the direction of desire will indicate in what direction each is most enriched. He who desires material gain will receive it, whilst he who desires spiritual gain will receive it. The real matter then to be weighed is—who is most benefited? Whose example is most beneficial to their fellow-creatures? Whether is treasure in the temporal earth-state, or treasure in the eternal, most desirable? To ask a man which he would prefer, would be the best way of beginning a transaction of the kind, if only a truthful reply could be got, but that is the difficulty. Some men make stock in trade of peculiar theories which have either originated in themselves or are borrowed from others. Everything which can be explained away or be bent to conform to their favourite theory is to them, being a gratification of self, as gain, and the desire of mind which leads such men to attribute selfish meanings to pure spiritual sayings in order to make them conform to their theories, may doubtless contribute to their stock in trade of self-glorification, and may even be made to appear very plausible to others, but it cannot in any way reflect the "Spirit of Truth." In language there is often a divergence of thought from the meaning intended to be conveyed, by the words actually used. Thus, while a person may wish to call another a fool he may call him a very clever fellow, and the person addressed may either infer that it was intended he should be called a fool, or, accepting the words literally, he may feel flattered. In the case of a man being called a fool who was not really such, he would be more likely to think it true than he who really was a fool would do. But then, there is a wide difference in the sense in which the word fool may be used. So is it with many other words and sentences. In fact, no language can, strictly speaking, convey the exact meaning intended to all minds alike. It is, therefore, utterly hopeless to found emphatic precept upon language, as every mind has a gauge of its own, and the only effective way, if any were possible, to convey strictly correct impressions would be, first to understand the individual gauge of mind and then to administer accordingly, and it is needless to say, that where the action of the mind is hid, as it is between men in the body, it is utterly impossible to know that gauge, or establish any uniformity of conception in thought by any prescribed form of language. As language is the expression of thought between men, and as thought enlarges its limits according to its experiences, some men will have thoughts beyond the capacity of their language, while the capacity of other minds will be inferior to the language they hear or read. Language, therefore, approximates to mental enlightenment or the reasoning powers, and these are based upon the impressions received through the senses. By revelation, however, man's knowledge can be increased as in no other way, for it comes of a wider range of observation by enlarged senses, and is knowledge, therefore, beyond his power to acquire in any other way. In illustration of the divergence of thought which occurs from the use of a few simple words, let us take the meanings which may be taken from the words "Might is Right." Few will acquiesce in the fitness of the principle involved in this expression in its application to matters of every-day life, and yet it is the principle under which differences between nations are settled even in this our day. The nation which musters the greatest power carries its points. "Might is right" represents truth under say three divergences of thought, each divergence exhibiting a particular growth of mind having a religion fitted to its comprehension. In the first of these divergences, the individual conscientiously believes that "might is right." He believes that God put him specially into his position of wealth and power, and made all men his slaves. This is a crude, low form of truth, and was found where a few half-enlightened men possessed the general wealth and power, and the masses were held in servile slavery and ignorance. This phase of thought coincides with the primitive religions of the Old Testament. The mind of the people was wrapt up in material gain, and the religion of the time appealing to this phase of mind required free offerings of the first-fruits, and the religious man yielded in them what he held most precious. In the second divergence of thought upon these words "might is right," man rises a little higher in the scale and in his conceptions of truth. He has emancipated his slaves and settled down into so-called civilised life, and he now conscientiously believes that slavery is wrong and that all men should enjoy equal rights. In this stage of thought he is convinced that he should maintain these principles, even if he fights to the death to enforce them upon others who think differently. "Does he not owe a duty to society, to his country, and to his God?" And, argues he, how could these prosper if he did not establish right, according to his view, even by the taking away of life, if necessary. This second phase of thought coincides with the religions which represent that the sacrifice of Christ's body was necessary in order that his blood might blot out the sins of the repentant—religions whose priests have not hesitated to consecrate the banners of men going to war with each other, in order that their churches might flourish. In the third divergence of thought upon the words "might is right," man's mind may, happily, rise to that higher conception of truth to which it was Jesus' aim it should rise, and to which we would wish it to rise, by man recognising in the laws of nature, and fully believing that "might is right" only when applied to God. The only sacrifice which this divergence of thought can believe in, as truly acceptable to God, is the sacrifice of all selfish inclinations, by the consecration of the every action of the mind to the will of the Father, making all things else subservient to that will. John iv. : "The hour cometh, and now is, when the true worshippers shall worship the Father in spirit and in truth." And as, by the laws governing revelation, no mind can have enforced upon it other matter than its growth, organisation, and desires admit of, so should man see that it is a violation of God's will to try to enforce his convictions upon others against their wishes. If it be asked, what evidences are found in nature to uphold the supremacy of the forms of truth represented in the third divergence of thought, which recognises that "might is right" only when applied to God, it may be answered, that force should reside where there is the greatest wisdom to guide it—that in the designs and operations of nature are unfolded a profundity of mind, harmony, and consistency which are to be traced alone to Divinity, and which are not approached by Scripture revelations received through the more or less prejudiced mind of man, or any other source known, for the wisest man cannot make even so much as a living leaf, and the most loving and constant would not send rain and sunshine upon friend and foe alike, nor exist unselfishly entirely for all others. Admitting the overwhelming testimony which nature bears to Supreme intelligence residing in the God of nature,—to God being more correctly revealed through nature than in any other way, and that nature is therefore our best guide—and, that God being the source of all wisdom, should also be recognised as the source of all power,—

it may be inquired, what are those particular evidences in nature which teach that the largest amount of wisdom, happiness, and power is attained by every action of our mind being brought into conformity with Divine will? In considering this, it becomes necessary to define what are our highest conceptions of Deity; for, as these should represent as near an approach to perfection as possible, it is obviously man's first duty to learn what are the principles of Divine existence and manifestation, in order that his life and actions may conform as closely as possible thereto. The writer, then, regards God as a great, all-permeating, infinite mind, nowhere seen personally, or in other words, His personality is not confined to one place, but is everywhere present, and expressed through all things according to their growth and requirements; and the lesson he would take from this is, that not only should it be the whole aim of men to work together for others, but that in doing so they should never seek to gain praise by allowing "self," or their personality, to be seen in their efforts for good. But, it may be asked, what is the character of that process in nature by which Deity is always administering unerringly to the requirements of all His creatures? The opinion entertained is, that, by the fixed properties or attributes given to matter and life, through their mind-wants or aspirations, they draw from the Infinite mind so much of intelligence and truth as they are susceptible of utilising, and for insuring general progression or increase; and the property of magnetic attraction, or affinity, which characterises all things in degree, from celestial movements to terrestrial objects, whether in matter or mind, is the law in nature through which wants are supplied. The mind of man is within the magnetic influence of the Infinite mind, as well as all other things, and by means of the attraction of desire man draws his supplies, spiritual or material, according to the direction of those desires. Thus God, as the answerer of prayer in all forms, is believed to be constantly administering to the requirements of all things; and if there be evidence of this nature of things, there cannot occur either that wasteful superfluity, such as the enforcement of advanced thought against the wishes of His creatures would represent, nor can there occur any unnatural direction or stint in His administrations, such as that represented by the father who, when asked for bread, would give his son a stone. The destruction of ferocious animals, and of the lower forms of animal life suited to the earlier history of the world, and the progress of mind through the higher types of life, and the general settlement and progress of enlightened mind on the world, shows that wants are supplied, for wants are progressive, and it is but one step further to credit the Infinite mind as the source of supply. According to habit of thought, it may be inferred that there is neither love nor wisdom of design in the laws of nature under which the ferocious and lower types of animal life have to give way to the higher types. It must be remembered, however, that death is but sleep—that there is no waste of matter, while the mind with its experiences lives again in a higher form of animal with better organisation, and in this manner the progression of mind on earth becomes manifest by the growing superiority of the organisms in material life upon it—hence, both the love and wisdom of the design become apparent to our reason. There is not only force represented in matter by that property through which its atoms or molecules are moved or attracted towards each other, but there is also mind represented in matter by that property through which those atoms can discriminate so as to form certain invariable combinations and disunites, just as man discriminates as to what combinations are best suited for his mind and body, i.e., what food he shall eat, what air he shall breathe, or what subjects shall occupy his mind, just as the lower animals and vegetable life select as to what combinations suit them best. It is very hard, however, to discriminate between the causation of force and mind ; for, while the magnetism with which all things are endowed gives them motion by reason of the affinity or attraction which atoms have for each other, it also gives a mind or method to that motion, and this mind harmonises all movements in nature. Mind and force, or knowledge and power, would appear to be given to all matter : and as magnetic attraction or force is only a phase of desire or want, all things must necessarily have wants of some kind ; and it is well they have, or there could be no progression, for it is this law of want, or force, by which mind and life are visibly expressed in matter. The force represented by magnetic affinity is not like the force which is obtained by man through mechanical appliances, for there is no visible machinery, as this force is simply a property of magnetic mind, which itself is unseen. It may be supposed, therefore, that the magnetic attraction, to which all force and motion is traced, is but a function of magnetic mind, and the means through which mind expresses itself through visible nature ; for matter remains the same, only changing its combinations, while force is used by mind intelligently to direct those changing combinations. This line of reasoning, if applied as a lesson of life, would lead to the inference that, after all, there is no labour or force so powerful or productive as that of mind ; and when we consider the immense amount of labour represented by the various processes to which steam and other machinery, the product of mind invention, is placed, and the immense influence which leading minds like that of Jesus, or in our own time that of Thomas Carlyle or J. S. Mill, exercise over mankind, the conclusion would appear to be pretty nearly correct. If it be assumed, therefore, that all matter obtains its motion from the mind with which it is endowed, and that mind uses motion with which to express itself through matter, the phases of light, heat, and electricity, as the equivalents of motion, as well as every phenomenon or condition of visible and invisible nature, may be directly traced to the majesty of the infinite controlling mind of God. When it is said matter is unchanging, except in its combinations—and when, at the same time, it is admitted that all matter is but the congregation of atoms, which, when separated, are too small to be visible to the naked eye—and, in addition to this, when all phenomena in visible nature are attributed to mind investing matter with certain properties—it may be asked, Were mind and matter co-existent? or, Are they mutually dependent upon each other? The opinion entertained is, that the All-pervading Spiritual Intelligence, which we call God, was ever-existent, and that matter is but forms of expression of His mind. The universe is but the body in which His mind resides and expresses itself, and His creatures are but parts of His body, just as the globular corpuscles which compose the blood which circulates in our veins are members of our body. [It is said that so infinitesimally small are those little creatures, that upon the point of the finest needle there may be lifted no less than 3,000,000, and each of them, let it be considered, is a living being, the habitation of mind.]   The universe, too, it is held, is endowed with life, sustained through the properties given to matter, and the Infinite mind that inspires it.   Matter, it is held, therefore, was not co-existent with mind, but was given out from mind, and it can be resolved by the magnetic fire of the Infinite mind back again into mind.

> " The cloud-capp'd towers, the gorgeous palaces,
>   The solemn temples, the great globe itself,
>   Yea, all which it inherit, shall dissolve ;
>   And, like the baseless fabric of a vision,
>   Leave not a rack behind.
>   We are such stuff as dreams are made on,
>   And our little life is rounded with a sleep."
> —*Shakespeare.*

In the higher types of life the organisms are more elaborate and perfect, coresponding with the advanced condition of mind—and in man, for instance, there is a dual condition, namely, the material and the spiritual nature, both with their necessary wants.   Man's body, indeed, represents the highest type, condition, or combination which atoms in this material life appear to be susceptible of forming.   Man may live, so to speak, between the material and spiritual worlds ; and so soon as his mind, by its experiences between these, leads him to turn his chief desires from drawing about him low worldly things for the temporary gratification of the animal nature, and to direct his aspirations to the perfection of his spiritual being, by living in harmony with nature according to the will of God, his mind is ripened for a still higher life in a spiritual body.   In this condition, the force of desire used by the mind is attractive to spiritual influences, and must, therefore, be relatively repulsive to low material influences.   Lord Bolingbroke, in his " Reflections upon Exile," says—" Our natural and real wants are confined to narrow bounds, while those which fancy create are confined to none ; " and the correctness of the conclusion is more apparent while there are around us so many slaves to habit and false appetite—drunkards, opiumeaters, smokers, and men who have, through a weakness in copying social habits, or otherwise, created low artificial cravings, or by satiety have allowed their ordinary animal desires to gain the mastery over the nobler aspirations of their spiritual being. When will man come to realise that by the purity of mind-desire, he may attract high spiritual influences, and a sufficiency of strength from God for any emergency, whilst by yielding to indulgences he attracts low influences, and his material nature becomes increasingly degenerate, and more and more estranged from his spiritual nature? Man's highest duty is to become pure in mind; and the more he exercises his mind in that direction, the stronger it becomes to resist evil. Donne remarks—

"He that makes one step up a stair, though he be not much nearer to the top of the house, yet he has stepped from the ground, and is relieved from the foulness and dampness of that. So, in this first step of prayer—O Lord, be merciful unto me—though a man be not established in heaven, yet he has stepped from the world and the miserable comforters thereof."

On our soul or mind is recorded all the desires of a lifetime, and our departed friends who may take an interest in our well-being by the action of our mind—which may be read by them—can see every passing thought, and the influence for good or bad which such thoughts may exercise on our spiritual being is by them well understood. Jesus seemed to recognise this law, for in Matt. chap. v., he is represented to have said, "Ye have heard that it was said by them of old time : Thou shalt not commit adultery. But I say unto you, that whosoever looketh on a woman to lust after her, hath committed adultery with her already in his heart." One of the finest teachings of Confucius was that people should always be on their guard and keep their innermost thoughts pure. Let those who are in the habit of speaking so glibly of their desire to reach, after death, a place which they call heaven, and who allude to the inestimable happiness of the angels, in which they hope to participate, consider well what is angel-life, and what is heaven. The belief here held is, that heaven is a condition as much as a place, and that it is made up of purity of mind and love. After death, if not before, it becomes most clearly apparent to our minds that those who devote their lives to the pursuit simply of material gratifications waste the opportunities of a life-time in pursuing an idle phantom. The material tastes, which were sent as a fire through which to try and prove the gold of the spiritual being and purify it, has been wasted, and the same ordeal will still have to be passed through. The mind, relieved of its animal instincts, clearly discerns that there is no real happiness except such as purity, wisdom, and love can bring to inward consciousness. Love, in the after-state, becomes the great causation of action ; and so the minds of the well-disposed become intensified with love after death. Hence, if man in this life desires fellowship with, and impression through the angel-world, he must place himself in affinity and harmony with them by seeing that all his desires, like theirs, are directed by pure and loving motives. Angel-life is a life devoted to exerting disinterested and loving influences amongst others, and the heaven and happiness of the angels is that condition of inward ecstatic joy which a consciousness of well-doing alone can bring. If all men would only regulate their motives according to this rule, there is nothing to prevent them from realising heaven with all its happiness upon earth. But while there is so much ignorance, with its evils, its misery, and its deformities, surrounding the loving and obedient, upon this world, they must only labour to improve mankind as best they can, and await their award in that happiness which comes to the good when their labours in the earth-life are brought to a close, and when, through death, they find that glorious entrance into light and life everlasting.

EXPERIENCES SUPPORTING THE CONCLUSIONS.

THE experiences which have been acquired, warrant the assertion that religion should be regarded in a different light from what it is at present by mankind generally. Instead of making it a thing to be dreaded and enforced, it should be regarded as a privilege of love to indulge in—a thing which will make people happy and noble, and not a thing calculated to degrade the mind under a belief of its criminality, and to make it for ever miserable, through standing in awe of impending punishment. Religion should not now be regarded as a thing based upon supernatural evidences, traditions, superstitions, and mystic ceremonials, nor upon unexplained laws, said to be no longer in operation, but it should be regarded as something definite, based upon revelation through natural laws at present at work, and upon the recognised evidences now existing in every department of nature, and which are consistent with the most profound researches of science. All that is good of Scripture is based upon the claim its best parts have to revelation and inspiration. If revelation was a fact in times past, it is a fact now. If it could teach men then, it can better teach men now. The religion of the day must be consonant with the revelation of the day. If there be no revelation and no inspiration now there never was any of either, and the claims held upon the authority of the Scriptures are worthless. It is here demonstrated, however, that the revelation and inspiration claimed for the Scriptures are based upon natural laws, now in operation, and these laws are now plainly indicated, and are thus made available for every-day use as a gauge within every one's reach, with which to distinguish truth from error. The time for basing spiritual beliefs upon mere tradition and upon things so called "supernatural" has gone by, and, seeing the amount of tyranny, and oppression, and ignorance that have prevailed under old beliefs so based, intelligent people are perfectly justified before God and man in asking for facts, at least, in evidence of theories.   If I were asked to believe a book, for which the claim of inspiration was held, I should read it and judge for myself, receiving what I could reasonably, but not necessarily receiving all or rejecting all because of the claim set up for the book, but I would weigh all, according to the intrinsic worth found in it, if any.   If I were asked to believe accounts furnished in such a book of some extraordinary spiritual phenomena, I should ask whether there be laws in nature rendering such phenomena possible; and if I found that such occurrences are known to people of the present time, under similar natural conditions, I would feel bound to acknowledge their truthfulness.   At any rate, such is the inference which any reasonable person may draw from such data.   It is held, therefore, that it is not enough to believe, but that we must have evidence of belief on which to base our suppositions, otherwise we labour under a blind belief.   Of the grand opening which shall be presented to us in the spirit state we know nothing, save what we have been told,—and that kind of evidence is now as open for appealing to as ever it was, and from precisely the same quarter may we hear of the future state, and under precisely the same conditions in nature,—the only and great distinction being, that each may obtain the evidence for himself, whereas each one has hitherto been receiving distorted and incorrect translations, of what *others have been said to have been told* of the future. Under these circumstances, it is obviously true that as people become more intelligent, and give more care to the things of the future, it will come to this, namely, that the prophecy of Jeremiah (of which Jesus reminds us), will be substantially verified, and " all men will be taught of God."

It has been advanced in this work that, according as a man exercises his mind desires for good or evil, so does he improve his being,—so does he develop, and so does he grow more capable ; and that the mind is self-recording, and that after the death of the body the mind lives still, and it is self-judging and self-rewarding.   It has also been advanced that in the body man's innermost thoughts and desires may be read and understood by unseen intelligence, and that man may be impressed or inspired for good or evil while he is in the body, according to his associations and the condition of affinity or direction of the desires of his mind for good or evil. An effort has been made, also, to indicate the nature of those laws in nature under which spiritual and Divine teaching may be received by man, and the conditions which are necessary to be observed in order to make a proper use of those laws. And it has been held that if people really so desire, they may now appeal in the same way to the same unerring source of instruction, as is so strongly advocated throughout the whole of the Old Testament and New Testament, and may now draw from that unerring source, God the Father, unerring truth, and that thus only will they be able to distinguish true revelation from false, human, and erroneous teachings, whether in Scripture or elsewhere. These are days of cool, deliberate, and serious reflection and inquiry, and people are learning to ask for evidence and reasons. If I say, then, that I believe in many of the spiritual phenomena mentioned in Scripture,—if I believe, in short, in spiritual communion, in visions, in revelation, prophecy, trance, cures, and inspiration, and that a certain unexplained force can be exercised by unseen intelligence, and that all these phenomena are governed by natural laws, as much now in operation as ever they were in Scripture times, I may very naturally and reasonably be asked to particularise circumstances and state facts relating to and occurring in our own times which would support such belief, and this is just what I propose here to do. In the first place, then, while in Canada some thirty-one years ago, I was one day walking along a well-lighted passage, in broad daylight, in my parents' own residence. In passing a door which opened into this passage, and which was at the time ajar, it was violently struck, as if by the fist of a powerful man. Not any one was near at the time, but to satisfy myself that no deception was being practised, I immediately sprang to the door, and after looking closely around to see that no one was at hand, I held it half-open and posted myself immediately facing the edge, holding the door between my two hands, and thus, with one eye in view of each side, I took up my position. Scarcely had this been done, when another violent blow was struck on the door immediately opposite to my face, and as near as could be judged within nine inches in front of my eyes, making the door shake. I was by myself at the time, and it was a beautiful sunshiney day. There had been for days and nights previous, a great variety of manifestations in this house, consisting mostly of knocks, bell-ringing, and clock-striking, which all in the house were anxious to find the cause of, but without avail, as all search proved fruitless. The simple occurrence just related was evidence to my mind, 1st, Of an unseen intelligence wishing to fix my attention ; 2d, An unseen intelligence being aware of my anxiety to have the blow repeated under close observation ; 3d, The exercise by an unseen intelligence of an unexplained force which did not require darkness as a condition of its manifestation. It may be asked, Why was my attention sought to be fixed by such a means? This question is best answered by other questions. Why, for instance, was the attention of the Fox family attracted by like means? Why did any of the spiritual phenomena with which Scripture abounds, take place? A few days after the occurrence just related had taken place, my sister was going out, and I accompanied her to the hall-door. It was about mid-day of a beautiful clear day. There was a flower-garden in front of the house, which was enclosed with a high wall from the street. The door through this wall, which led through the garden to the hall-door, invariably made a noise which could be heard when it was opened or shut. Just as we got to the hall-door the bell was pulled from the outside. Not having heard the outer gate make a noise, and not hearing any footstep outside, we looked at each other in astonishment, as much as to say, "Was this the ghost again?" for all such things used to be put down to ghostly influences in those days. The door, however, was suddenly opened by us, but no one was there. The door was closed again, and we having posted ourselves behind it, my sister exclaimed : "It is the ghost! That is not loud enough. Perhaps you will ring a little louder." The bell was at once pulled stronger, and having a hand on the door ready it was instantaneously opened, but not a person nor cause could be discovered. We shut the door, and again posted ourselves on the inside, ready to open it quickly. My sister then exclaimed :—"That was not half loud enough ; why can't you ring louder?" when immediately it was pulled in such a way we thought the wire would have been broken. The door was again instantaneously opened, but no person nor cause could, this time either, be discovered, although my sister, being first, said she thought she noticed like the shadow of a hand on the bell-pull, but, as I judge for myself, if it was so, it faded too soon for me to see it. She then exclaimed : "That is enough of that nonsense, we don't want any more of it." We had, up to this time, been much concerned with the singular manifestations that had been so continuously taking place in the house, but, it was remarked, that from that time there was not any repetition of them. In these phenomena we have again the unseen intelligence seemingly anxious to teach us the possibility of communion with the spirit-world ; we have it answer the requests made, by pulling louder and louder, and finally desisting altogether when so requested ; besides, we have the exercise of a certain amount of unexplained force in broad daylight. Upon one occasion in childhood I was told, while in sleep at night, that I would find two pennies covered up in about a shovelful of sweepings in a part of a yard attached to my parents' dwelling which was not generally used as a place for depositing sweepings. Remembering the dream, I went on the following morning to the spot indicated, and, sure enough, there found the sweepings and turned up the pennies, yet no one was found to explain whose they were nor how they got there. This was evidently a spiritual communication by some one closely in affinity. While referring to the recollections of youth I will here parenthetically state two peculiar incidents, although they have little relation to experiences bearing upon the phases of belief indicated. It is singular how some minds are very strong in recollecting certain things, such as incidents, while they may be very poor at remembering names and figures, and others will be quite the reverse. I have always been good at recollecting circumstances, and many have doubted the correctness of my statement when I have told them that my memory brings me back to a time when I was only an infant in my mother's arms and had not commenced to speak. I remember one occasion then, when I was in great pain and was crying bitterly on account of it. On that occasion, my mother, to soothe my troubled soul, as mothers will do, began to rock and to sway my diminutive carcase in her maternal arms. That swaying, however, only increased my pain, and here is the remark-

K

able part of the affair : I remember the pain and all the surroundings of the occasion, and I remember distinctly regretting my inability to make her understand my wishes, and to comprehend that such dandling, however affectionately intended, was really increasing the discomfort. A Baptist minister, who is now about seventy years of age, and with whom I am personally acquainted, affirms deliberately that he recollects the time he was weaned from his mother's breast. Contrasting this with my own experience, there does not appear to be much difference in the force of recollection between us, although, phrenologically speaking, he appears to have come into the world with a larger development of alimentiveness. Before I had given much consideration to the subject of the reincarnation of mind into two or more bodies in man, I recollect being told by a German magnetic trance-medium that my mind had been reincarnated in no less than fourteen different bodies as man on this earth ; that my last bodily experience was in the condition of a well-to-do English American ; and that my previous bodily experience was in the condition of a much-abused slave about a palace in Sweden, I think; that I had always been delicate, my average life being under forty years ; but that I had had an earthly existence as man before the Flood, and that the Flood alluded to in Scripture had not covered the whole world, but merely certain portions of Asia Minor. I am not in a position to contradict the medium in question, but, assuming correctness, is it possible that the sagaciousness acquired in my American experience is sufficient to account for the precociousness of the infant ? The other matter which I have undertaken parenthetically to refer to here has reference to Canada, and a time when the very foundations were being laid for the inauguration of those admirable systems of liberal responsible government, which the more important of the British colonies now enjoy. Mr. Papineau, in Canada, had demanded the election of a second chamber, but that, with other demands, was frustrated by a Royal Commission, whose head was Lord Gosford. After this, and in consequence of an attempt made by the Imperial Parliament to seize the money which the Canadian Parliament refused to vote to defray the expenses of the Government, a rebellion was commenced with which Mr. Papineau was connected.

While the rebels were mustering their forces, and were marching past my parents' residence, shouting, "Hurrah for Papineau!" it is related by my mother and elder sisters, that, while then only an infant in arms and not yet commenced to articulate, I was taken to the window to see the crowd, when I joined in the cry and said, "Hurrah for Papineau!" which extraordinary beginning at talking may, perhaps, account for the fact that I have never since been able to speak well! Mr. Papineau died at his residence at Montebello, on the Ottawa, a year or two ago, and a leading Canadian newspaper concludes an obituary notice of him in the following terms:—

"Mr. Papineau was the O'Connell of Canada, and, indeed, of all the British colonies. He laid the foundation, so to speak, of responsible government in the province, and he lived to see the working of the reforms which he had so often and so vigorously agitated. A noble man, a great man, and an honest man ; his name will live while the Canadian nation has an existence, though his example as an agitator is not one to be followed."

The point to be considered is, was it really I who spoke thus for the first time, or was I impressed to speak, or was it a case of "possession," where another intelligence exercises the organism of, or speaks through, the body belonging to another mind? My first experience at spiritual seances, for table manifestations, was gained several years ago. While spending an evening in a friend's house, one of the company jocularly proposed that we should try a spirit circle, and the party agreeing, about nine of us sat around a table. As none of the party had ever sat in "circle" before that, a little hesitation occurred as to how we should proceed; finally, one of our number having read how a "circle" was conducted, a day or two previous, undertook to direct us. Some of us tried to keep very quiet and solemn — one or two ladies, who at first were well enough behaved, after two or three minutes began to titter ; one gentleman, a few minutes later, became fussy and sceptical, and finally withdrew from the circle, protesting the thing to be all madness. After sitting fifteen minutes the table oscillated a little, when our director *pro tempore* said, "If any spirit is here it will please manifest its presence by rapping on the table twice." The raps were audibly given—and the table began to move to and fro with greater force.   The spirits were then requested to move the table towards the best medium present, and it moved very firmly and decidedly towards a lady next to me, who was then accordingly elected to put any questions. Several were put orally, and replies were rapped out—after which the table was moved in certain peculiar directions in response to some mental questions which had to be answered by movements in one of two particular directions. A question was then put which, if answered in the negative, was to be signified by a slight movement to left of the medium, but if answered in the affirmative, was to be signified by a movement to the extreme right side of the room, when the table took a clear run to the far right corner of the room, leaving all the sitters behind, except two, viz., the lady medium and myself, who had to rise from our seats and follow it.   At this stage of the proceedings the " circle " was, of course, entirely broken up, and we two, the only ones continuing to take further part, scarcely touched the table (which must have weighed forty pounds) with the tips of our fingers ; in fact, for some seconds at a time, our fingers did not even touch it.   Another question was now put, which, to be answered in the affirmative, rendered it necessary that the table should be tipped over, by this unseen agency, on its side upon the floor.   Strange to say, the table was so tipped over, and the edge of its top was rested gently upon the floor, the legs becoming horizontal and parallel with the floor, while the top was perpendicular to the floor.   Another question had to be put, and this required for an affirmative reply that the table should be lifted up again upon its legs properly on the floor ; and scarcely had it been put when the table righted itself without visible assistance.   This ended the evening's proceedings, but it commenced an earnest desire on my part to know more.   The manifestations thus witnessed were so obviously destitute of trickery, and still to me, as then, of such an incomprehensible nature, that they fairly awakened in me a spirit of inquiry.   In this case, we have evidence, again, in the intelligent replies received, of the presence of an unseen intelligence, and in the rappings and the movements of the table, we have evidence again of an unexplained force.   The theory of that force being due to a collection of animal magnetism from the sitters, will scarcely hold good, inasmuch as more force was exercised when there was no longer such a circle to collect that force from ; moreover, by the force of magnetism, we generally suppose the article moved will necessarily move in the direction of the magnet, whereas this force moved the table away from the sitters and their hands ; and the direction of the movements indicated that the control of the force was exercised by other intelligence, not observed in person. The clairvoyant powers exercised by some people are very remarkable. An instance is furnished in John i., where Nathanael having been pointed at by Jesus, as " an Israelite indeed, in whom is no guile," he asked him, " Whence knowest thou me? ' When Jesus replied, " Before that Philip called thee, when thou wast under the fig-tree, I saw thee." Whereupon Nathanael, in his astonishment at the exercise of such a power of vision, is represented to have exclaimed, " Rabbi, thou art the Son of God ; thou art the King of Israel."

I remember suffering from some internal complaint which some medical men consulted could not explain, and which was not by myself understood. Having been told of some remarkable cases in which persons by sending a few hairs cut from their heads to a clairvoyant, had received from him particulars as to the nature of their ailments with prescriptions which had proved efficacious, I resolved, by way of curiosity, to send a few hairs from my head, and, without much handling of them, enclosed them in a letter asking to be told what was wrong. Without seeing me, or having any personal knowledge of me, this healing clairvoyant-medium wrote back a clear exposition of my particular internal ailment, and gave a prescription through which I believe the complaint soon left me. An experienced physician, who had been incapacitated for some time from following his profession through not being able to move about, and who could not find any relief through his own knowledge or that of other medical men whom he had consulted, is known to have been cured in the same way through this medium. A lady who was suffering from agonising pains in the head, and who could get no relief from skilled practitioners, is known also to have been cured by this clairvoyant. Besides these cases, a very large number of persons, suffering from various complaints which had not been successfully treated by regular medical men, are known to have been cured in like manner. I once met a woman who by the work of her own hands, in industry, was making a scanty but honest living. She professed to have "the gift of healing." She used to invite together a number of persons who wanted to be cured. She would read to them from 12th, 13th, and 14th chapters of 1st Corinthians, as also from parts of the gospels where "gifts of healing," &c., were promised. On one occasion in my presence, in simple language, she said she not only believed in those promises, but she had received the power of healing (and she told of the circumstances under which she received it, or had become aware that she had it), and she had exercised that power (and she furnished the names, addresses, and particulars of ailments of a number of persons that had been cured through her); and, moreover, she declared that she was there before them to exercise this gift of healing without money or price to any that wished, whether believers or not, upon the one condition that they would give the glory to God if healed. Several of those present submitted themselves, in my presence, to be anointed by her in the name of God "through Christ," and some three or four persons were there who, in my presence, said they had come to acknowledge their gratitude for the goodness of God, inasmuch as they had been cured of complaints they had previously suffered from through the instrumentality of this woman, who had anointed them at a previous gathering. This is substantially "primitive Christianity," as presented to us in the New Testament. If so-called "Christians" deny the possibility of the exercise of such gifts, they necessarily show they have no real belief in what they profess to believe. How was this woman treated by the so-called Christian daily press? There was a reporter present at that meeting, but, to his credit be it remarked, he was not a witness to the statements of those who testified to having been cured, as they came forward with their statements after he had left the room; the consequence was that, in the next morning's paper, the meeting was noticed in a sneering paragraph, in which the woman was ridiculed, and "humbug" was imputed to her. When John complained to Jesus that he had found a man who was doing great things in his name, and that he had rebuked him because that he would not follow them, Jesus said : " Forbid him not, for he that is not against us, is for us." Although the quaintly-written epistles of Paul present a singular jumble of truth and error intermixed, which may be held largely accountable for many extravagant beliefs which prevail in Christian churches, and which are not warranted under the teachings of Jesus, yet those writings exhibit in places an intimate acquaintance with the laws of God. He says in one part :

" There must be also heresies among you, that they which are approved may be made manifest among you." Again he says: " For we know in part, and we prophesy in part, but when that which is perfect is come, then that which is in part shall be done away." " The head of every man is Christ," and " the head of Christ is God." " Ye are the body of Christ, and members in particular." " To one is given the spirit of wisdom, to another the gifts of healing, to another prophecy, to another discerning of spirits, to another divers kinds of tongues, but all these worketh that one and the self-same Spirit, dividing to every man severally as he will. For, as the body is one, and hath many members, and all the members of that one body, being many, are one body, so also is Christ."

These teachings accord closely with Jesus' teaching of at-one-ment. In John 6th, 7th, and 8th chapters, Jesus is represented to have said :

" The words that I speak unto you, they are spirit and they are life." " No man can come unto me, except it were given unto him of my Father." Peter said, " To whom shall we go ? Thou hast the words of eternal life." Some time after this Jesus went up to the Temple and taught, and the Jews marvelled, saying, " How knoweth this man letters, having never learned ? " Jesus said, " My doctrine is not mine, but His that sent me. If any man will do His will, he shall know of the doctrine, whether it be of God, or whether I speak of myself. He that speaketh of himself, seeketh his own glory ; but he that seeketh his glory that sent him, the same is true." " I do nothing of myself, but as my Father hath taught me, I speak these things. He that sent me is with me. The Father hath not left me alone, for I do always those things that please Him."

When the mind ripens sufficiently to realise that the only wisdom and happiness worth having is that which can alone be obtained through a constant desire to do the will of the Father, and to live at-one with Him, the mind is then " drawn " of the Father, and can distinguish the doctrines of God from the selfish doctrines of man. So it is with tnese magnetic cures. It is not the medium that cures. The medium is simply used as a medium, through which the magnetic current may be. drawn down by natural law towards the person ailing, to restore, as it were, to healthful circulation some dormant vitalising element, the want of which occasioned trouble and suffering. The manifestations which had been witnessed at the impromptu circle held at my friend's house made me very anxious to know more of spiritualism. Accordingly, in my own house I formed a circle. Four or five members of my own family, all novices, had the kind assistance of a lady of good mechanical writing and fair impressional mediumship. We were all desperately in earnest to learn of truth. The circle was very successful, and some very interesting and instructive writings were received. At one of our first sittings, in a lengthy message written by the lady medium under mechanical conditions, it was stated that I was then suited for mechanical writing, and would soon develop to be an inspirational medium ; and in a very short time I got intelligible mechanical writings, both in circle and privately by myself. I became so enthusiastic over these writings that, in ignorance of the consequences, I sat too frequently by myself, although I was frequently warned in those writings not to sit so frequently. The consequence was the nerve-current in my system became seriously disturbed, and the action of my heart and the blood-circulation were impeded, and I became very unwell, and was for a considerable time laid up in bed, and had to seek medical advice. The doctors did not know what to make of me. The organs of the body were sounded on different occasions by four or five practitioners, but nothing wrong was discovered ; nevertheless, the pulse was scarcely to be felt. I took their medicines, but they did no good. At last one day, as I was in bed and very bad, it occurred to me that I might get a remedy by mechanical writing mediumship. Accordingly, getting hold of my pocket-book, I tried, and received a written prescription by simply holding a pencil-point lightly on the surface of the paper, and allowing my hand and arm to be easily moved. My hand with pencil was by this means moved by unseen intelligence, and by an unexplained force, in broad daylight, in such a way as to cause to be written a prescription giving the names and proportions of two ingredients, of the medicinal properties of which I was ignorant. That prescription was taken to a druggist, and he, being asked if the proportions, &c., were correct, referred to the "British Pharmacopœia," and stated they were. The medicine was accordingly taken, and within a few days I was well and improving in strength. This is again evidence surely of unseen intelligence and communion, and the exercise of an unexplained force. An explanation of the manner in which the disturbance is supposed to take place in the system is given in a previous portion of this work thus: "The arm and hand are moved to write by means of an external current of magnetism, applied by spiritual agency to the nerves of the arm and hand, and this current not coming through the regular channel of the brain motor, interrupts the natural nerve-current generated in and circulating through the body." Upon one occasion, while sleeping in a building by myself, I was awakened about midnight by a violent jerking of the muscles of the right arm; it disturbed me from a very sound sleep at the time. Not realising that it was anything beyond a nervous disturbance, I turned around on the other side, and tried to get off to sleep again. Scarcely, however, had I thus settled myself, than my arm was again violently jerked. This time, being awake, I understood from previous experiences that something was wanted of me. Accordingly I arose from bed, got a light and paper and pencil, and by mechanical mediumship my hand was at once moved to write:—"You are in danger, the wall is giving way." Immediately after, I heard a crack in a wall alongside of which my bed was placed. It was raining at the time, and it was a very disagreeable night out of doors. That did not prevent me from obeying the advice, however, for, without further delay, I dressed and sought quarters in a hotel in the neighbourhood. Some new buildings had just been erected at the back of the premises in which I had been sleeping, and on making inquiries next morning I found that a tunnel had been driven in order to drain the new buildings towards the street, and it then became apparent for the first time, upon examination, that a mistake had been made by the builders giving a wrong direction to the tunnel, whereby the foundation of the wall against which I had been sleeping was completely undermined.   The contractors, on being questioned, immediately discovered the mistake made, and recognising the necessity of the work, they gave orders to their men to secure the foundation, and the wall was at once secured.   With evidences like these before me, how can I doubt the loving watchfulness and care with which my every movement is guarded?   At this time, I still continued my own family circle, and I found, while following the mechanical medium- ship moderately, that I was rapidly developing as an impressional medium.   It came about in this way : whereas at first I had no knowledge, through my mind, of what my hand was about to be moved to write, after a while such knowledge came through my mind, first, by a single word at a time, and then by two or more words, until at length I was impressed with in some cases a whole sentence before writing.   Mechanical mediumship, from this stage, was no longer necessary, and therefore was not resorted to ; while Impression or Inspiration was more and more cultivated, both in private writing, and for obtaining advice by mental interrogation on matters of spiritual concern, whether arising in family or in business matters in every-day life, but more especially in such matters as by the ordinary senses one could not distinguish as to the immediate results of.   In such cases, one must be prepared to follow the course one way or other just as under the teaching of Jesus, not to his own inclination but to the glory of God.   "Not my will, but thine be done."   " Even so, O Father," we must be prepared to say, "may the course to be recommended to us thus seek- ing light from thee, be under thine infinite knowledge and love, in accordance with THY WILL."   At about this stage of my experiences there was a very strong circle of spiritualists being held at the house of a neighbour, for the purpose of developing speaking, particularly under the trance and possession phases.   Being invited, I attended it for some time, and heard, under possession, some very good sound addresses ; I also heard a lady sing the words and music of hymns that were, so far as the knowledge of all present was concerned, perfectly new and original.   As this circle did not appear to assist my further development I ceased to attend it, and shortly after, through a desire to put others upon a road which had ushered in so much hope to my mind that was before unknown to it, I organised some large circles for mechanical and impressional writing. After this I attended a magnetic class for the development of impressional writing, and this kind of mediumship it has been my constant desire to attend to ever since. While persevering with this phase of mediumship I have at times, while sitting alone under favourable conditions, received whole pages of matter inspirationally—matter dictated to me word by word through my brain as I wrote it down, the ideas and arguments being obtained without any effort of mind, memory, or thought, and being in themselves perfectly new to me. There is one thing which my experience of inspiration has led me to notice very particularly, and that is this, the force and quality of inspiration is governed by certain unalterable laws of God's nature, and to seek pure inspiration without conforming to those laws one might as reasonably expect that water would flow uphill of itself. The greatest drawback to obtaining pure impression is the nursing in the mind of unworthy motives, such as a desire to defraud or to injure any one in any way, to bear revenge, hatred, or have any evil or low design either as against any one else or as against the individual bodily organisation, which should always be regarded as "the temple of the living God," and should accordingly be kept pure and undefiled. I have invariably noticed inspiration to come pure and strong in seasons of obedience to the Father; when I have been in bodily health; when I have taken a wholesome walk on the tops of country hills, through majestic forest trees, and through beautiful and refreshing flower-gardens, or by the sea-side; or when I have walked along the banks of a fine river, in one part still, deep, and solemn, in another widening out into a shallow and troubled course, washing boulders and rocks, and in another leaping, it may be, from a great precipice into a deep abyss, darkened by overhanging rocks and trees, to find its way out in other parts, beautiful and gushing and living as ever; or when my mind has been taken up with an earnest unselfish design of doing good to others. These are the times, the conditions, and the circumstances under which, as man looks up from nature to nature's God, he drinks in of the purest and highest of inspirations. While persevering in my endeavours, under more or less favourable circumstances, to obtain higher

truths through inspiration, it has been my lot to experience
a great variety of spiritual phenomena, some of which I will
endeavour to give a brief account of.   Upon one occasion,
for instance, as I was sleeping in a building by myself, at
about midnight, a verse of poetry, in broad Scotch, after the
style of Burns, was recited to me by some unseen spiritual
agency, and as my sleep was but light, I mentally suggested
the inquiry whether it would not be much better to render
such poetry in proper English language.   Scarcely had such
idea been mentally conceived by me than a verse expressing similar sentiments was immediately recited in good plain
English, rhyme and metre.   This strange coincident had
the effect of completely arousing me, and, arising from my
bed and getting a light and paper and pencil, I thereupon
received, by impressional dictation, several verses of poetry
without further expenditure of time than was necessary to
enable me to perform the mere mechanical labour of writing
the lines down.   Many cases are known in our time where,
by spiritual or unseen intelligence, revelations have been
made at the self-same time to persons of important occurrences happening in far-off parts to others with whom
they have been on intimate terms.   I will recite a strange
case of the kind, but the people whose action was revealed
through me had never been seen by me and were perfectly
unknown to me.   While residing at a place distant about
sixteen thousand miles from London, I had a youth in my
employ.   This youth had a relative who had left the
country, in quite an unexplained manner, for some other
part quite unknown.   By " accident " one day, while his
mother was speaking to a new arrival from England, she
happened to mention the singular departure of their relative, when, strange to say, this new arrival had met the
very person alluded to under another name in London ;
and, what is stranger, had just left that relative's employ
there.   Thinking it just possible they had really found out
in this unexpected way their relative, the youth wrote to
the address indicated, and, as weeks and months of time
passed on, the incident was quite forgotten.   One morning,
as I was getting up for the business of the day at my usual
time, and was engaged in the process of arranging my
personal attire, a spirit voice unexpectedly whispered
in my ear the following words with great clearness :—

"A letter with money in it, has been sent to you from England." I was not thinking of anything in the most remote degree connected with such a subject at the time; moreover, I had no relations, nor friendly or business correspondents in England, and the thing seemed so utterly improbable that I at once discredited it. Nevertheless, these words had come so utterly unexpected, and with such great clearness, I immediately took a note of them and the date in my diary. Had not my mind been excited, so soon as it realised these first words conveying a definite impression, I have every reason to suppose words might have continued to flow and have shaped themselves with fuller meaning. Be that as it may, their meaning was certainly not understood nor suspected at that time. About two months after this occurrence my youth was surprised at the receipt, through post to my care, of a money-letter from his long lost relative, who, sure enough, proved to be the person written to in London. By this time I had quite forgotten about the spirit-whisper, and the entry made of it. About four weeks after this, in the course of business conversation with some gentlemen, I had occasion to refer to my diary for a date, when my eye caught the entry of the notable spirit-whisper, and I for the first time realised the whole affair. Forgetting the business in hand, I at once turned to the youth and appealed to him as to the date of the letter he had received. Having it in his pocket, he referred to it, and the date corresponded exactly to the time of that spirit-whisper within a day, which, allowing for the difference in the longitude between the two places and the posting, would just be accounted for. At one time my mind very foolishly was too much occupied with thoughts of mining enterprises. One night during sleep I was told to buy shares in a certain company, the name of which was clearly given, but the existence of a company of such a name was totally unknown to me. I tried to remember that name in my sleep. On getting up in the morning, I was reminded, first in a very indistinct manner, that a dream was to be remembered, then I recollected the impression I had received to buy shares in a certain company, but the name was forgotten; then, after a while, the name was remembered. So, on going to business, I made a point of referring to a published list of companies to see if any one of that particular name existed. Sure enough, the name was there, and there was only one of that name. Referring to the market quotations next, the shares were found to be 1s. 6d. on that day. I did not purchase any. The next day the shares went up, and the next, and next, for some time, until they reached 12s. per share. I never had much faith in appealing to such a source for the purpose of making money, and I have less faith now in it than I ever had, although in my early experience, it must be acknowledged, I did use it, and, on one occasion, it must be admitted that had I not attended promptly to a warning received, I should have lost a very large sum of money through the embezzlements of a manager and the failure of a mine. That magnetic currents operate between minds both in and out of the material body, it is assumed, may not only be demonstrated by the laws known to govern our physical natures, but may be inferred from the magnetic lights which at times have been observed by the inspired. In a previous portion of this work the influences exerted under electro-biological and other phases of phenomena have been referred to, in order to indicate that a connection of a powerful controlling character may be obtained between minds in the body, by the establishment of a magnetic current by means of passes and otherwise—and that impression itself is but a phase of such connection between mind in and out of the material body. I have myself, by request, operated upon persons electro-biologically, and, after making a few passes, realised the fact that the organisations of my subjects were completely under the control of my mind, in so far that my subjects would really believe and imagine anything which my mind communicated to them as being the case, although such communication might be obviously untrue to the observation of any other persons present who had the control of their own ordinary senses. For instance, a glass of cold water would be handed to the subject, and at first taste, if told by me that it was cold water, he would believe it ; at second taste, without leaving hold of the glass, if told by me it was hot water, he would believe it ; at third time, if told it was beautiful fresh milk, he would believe it by sight and taste ; at fourth taste, if told it was hot coffee, he would believe it ; and so on with wine, beer, or as many other drinks as he might be told the same cold water was he would believe. If with my finger I pointed to the hard floor, and told the subject that it was a pond of water, and that a child playing on the edge had fallen in, and would urge him to save the drowning child, he would at once plunge upon the hard floor, under the idea that he was saving a child from water. On the other hand, I have tested the power of animal magnetism under electro-biological conditions. A friend of mine on one occasion desired me to operate upon him, so, having got him stretched on the floor, I made passes down his body from head to feet, and his limbs were thus made rigid. Then, standing straddle over his body, and bending towards his feet with my arms and hands outstretched towards his ankles, but without absolutely touching them with so much as my finger-ends, I raised him from the floor rigid and straight, almost to an angle of twenty degrees, simply, so far as I could judge, by a strong exercise of will-power or by animal magnetism thus generated or applied. It has been asserted on more than one occasion that people have seen what have been called magnetic lights, and medical men have tried to make out that the lights so seen simply arose from a well-ascertained condition of the sight under which lights appear to float before the eyes. My experience leads me to believe that this explanation, however correct in itself as applied to a certain condition of the sight, will not hold good in all cases where lights have been observed. I scarcely ever sit down for inspirational writing without detecting a peculiar light for a moment visiting me, and often this comes like a flash across my face, while my eyes are fixed unmoved upon the writing. Sometimes, when impressed during the day in conversation, or while meditating, it will unexpectedly flash upon me. On a fine day, on one notable occasion, while walking with my son, I was conversing and explaining to him what enlarged opportunities mankind now enjoyed through the spiritual light which was being poured upon mind to ripen it, and how mind, in consequence of this outpouring, was now being emancipated from the cruel bonds of human tradition, in order that man might breathe-in, with greater freedom and joy, higher, purer, and more inspiring conceptions of Deity; and that henceforth man might, through the incentive alone of a purer love for God, without necessity for theories of punishments and rewards, live in harmony with all nature, and enjoy heaven upon earth. While thus speaking over these matters I was startled by distinguishing a powerful current of magnetic light, having the appearance of zig-zag lightning, descending upon us. A number of other phenomena, of more or less importance, have been experienced. On several occasions, for instance, I have smelt a peculiar delicious perfume, which, judged from the circumstances under which it has come, has been regarded as an expression of encouragement or approval. There was no confusing it with any other perfume that I happened to be aware of, and it has been experienced by others while in my company. On two or three occasions, at request, I have magnetised persons, by holding their hands and looking steadfastly into their eyes ; and, under these conditions, I have plainly distinguished other people, that I had no recollection of ever seeing before—people who might be in likeness either to their former selves, as before incarnated in another previous body, or their present impressors, but people bearing little or no resemblance to their natural selves. In my wife's case, for instance, I plainly saw a beautiful Egyptian lady, although she bears no appearance of the kind naturally. In some cases I have succeeded in making cures and relieving pain by making magnetic passes ; but this is very commonly done, I believe, with people. While travelling some years ago I met a person, and, in conversing, the subject of spiritualism was alluded to. He professed to know nothing about it, but was anxious to hear something, as he recollected a thing which had happened to himself in boyhood, which, although in itself of no importance, seemed to him unaccountable without there was communication between seen and unseen intelligence. He stated that in youth he was very fond of pigeons. He was at one time speculating how he could best catch some that constantly frequented his father's yard. There was a kind of porch in the yard. One night he dreamt he had devised a plan by which he had enticed a number of pigeons into the porch, that he had then rushed upon them, and succeeded in capturing two beauties of remarkable plumage. Next day, without recollecting the dream, he set to and carried out the same plan, and, rushing in upon the pigeons, he managed to catch one between his legs, while he succeeded at the same instant in catching another in a grab at full arm's length over his head, while it was with others making good its escape by flying out of the entrance. Proud of the capture, he held the birds there, one in each hand, to examine and admire them, when, for the first time, he was amazed not only at being reminded of his dream of the previous night, but at witnessing thus its complete verification so unexpectedly. There, in his hands were, sure enough, the selfsame birds that he had seen in the vision !

Paul, in 1st Corinthians xiv., says : "Follow after charity, and desire spiritual gifts, but rather that ye may prophesy." The so-called Christianity of our day is very inconsistent in many respects with its professions. It makes a great fuss about Paul's teachings ; and, although it will admit of no exceptions or exemptions from Bible teachings in general, and Paul's teachings in particular, yet, by some unexplained philosophy peculiar to the theological school, it will not sanction that we should "desire spiritual gifts," and as for "prophecy," any one who would, according to Paul, be so fortunate as to be able to acknowledge that he possessed this as the *best* of "spiritual gifts," would by theologians be regarded as a fit and proper person for excommunication from all the so-called Christian Churches in the land. The rank materialism of professing Christians keeps them blinded to the fuller meanings of all the very highest and most ennobling lessons of *pure* Christianity. They will only admit of such a thing as "prophecy" in the restricted sense, that coming events may be foretold only by means of observations and calculations made by reasoning upon causes known by man to be in operation. A man is walking under a high precipice, for instance, looking thoughtlessly upon the ground, quite unconscious of any danger. Another man from a distance observes a large stone to start from the summit of that precipice, and, from its downward course being towards the unobserving man, he may "prophesy" that, within so many seconds, that man will be killed by a falling stone. If professing Christians can take no larger view of prophecy than that, they simply give the lie to the finest prophecies of Scripture. For my part, I believe both in revelation and in prophecy

L

in their true sense ; and I call the "prophecy" of materialists nothing more than calculations or guess-work,—either
the product of human reasoning upon the observations of
the material senses, or else the mere expression of idle
imagination, intended to mystify or deceive. I will relate
a case or two within my own experience, which not only
establishes the possibility but the actuality of both revelation and prophecy in our own time. Some time ago, there
was in my employ a very fine young gentleman in robust
health. One night in sleep, in vision, there was presented
before my eyes a copy of a leading newspaper which had
printed in it a notice of the death of that young gentleman.
I was at his side at business almost every day ; and at that
time he was the very picture of health and vitality, and
without any ailment that was known of. The nature of
my vision was reported on the following day to my wife,
to himself, and to one or two others. He attended to business in perfect health for some days afterwards. Within a
month from the time of that vision he was invited to pay a
visit, with his wife, to some friends who resided a short
distance out of town. They went ; and while there it was
suggested they should go for a drive in a buggy with a pair
of ponies belonging to his friend. He went into the yard
to see the ponies harnessed ; and, in order to facilitate
matters, he raised the pole of the buggy, and was in the
act of wheeling it into its proper position, when he tripped
over a small stone, and, falling backward, the pole fell upon
his stomach and ruptured him so badly that he died
within a few hours, and a notice of his death actually
appeared in the same paper and form in which the vision
had presented it. That death could not have been foretold
by any purely human powers of observation, inasmuch as
it occurred by what is commonly called "pure accident."
A young daughter of my own, that had made herself very
much beloved from the natural extra goodness of her
character, took very ill a few days before my friend met
with his "accident." The medical man attending her
recommended a change of air, and she was removed.
Another medical man was then called in, and he recommended removal again as the "only chance," so she was
removed twice within a few days, and this last time she
was taken to friends who had no knowledge of her sick-

ness until she had arrived at their house. She died there two days afterwards, and that was within forty-eight hours after the death of my friend from the "accident." The lady of the house, who is a perfectly truthful person, knew nothing of my friend or the circumstances connected with his death, and she seriously affirmed, immediately after our daughter had died, that a friend of her own had divined a few days previously that "a strange child was to be brought to her house and would die there." While on a visit to Canada during the year 1875, I was invited to join in a fishing-party, for a one or two weeks' excursion among some beautiful lakes and rivers to the north and west of Quebec. One of our party was a Wesleyan minister; and I soon discovered that his mind had expanded far beyond the liberal limits of the tenets which those of his denomination profess to hold, although Wesley himself was a spiritist. I was told by another of the party who knew him intimately, that he generally preached extemporaneously from prepared heads; and, although in private he exhibited a want of ordinary power in language, he appeared in the pulpit, said he, to grow eloquent by inspiration in his sermons after commencing, and often gave expression to ideas which fairly staggered some of his orthodox hearers. We had one or two nice private chats together during our excursion; and when I asked his convictions on the theory of original sin and the other theories or plans of redemption and justification which had grown out of the theory of original sin, or the account furnished of that unfortunate fruit-dessert of which Mr. and Mrs. Adam are supposed to have partaken with such disastrous results to mankind in general, he almost at once fell into my views. Speaking of present revelation, clairvoyant powers, &c., he had reason on more than one occasion, it appeared, from incidents happening within his own personal experience, to believe in those phenomena. On one occasion, he stated, that in sleep he saw a young lady acquaintance of his writing a letter to him, and he both saw and read the contents of it, as it was written. The young lady was residing in another part of the town from him. Next day he visited her, and gave her an answer to it. She was alarmed, for the letter although written had never been delivered, and her sister, sharing a knowledge of that fact, produced the letter, which had been closed and addressed and put aside at the time, and was now found there still un-opened. He told her the full contents of that letter, to her utter astonishment. On another occasion, not long before we met, in a wild part of Canada in which he had been stationed, his ministerial labours necessitated his travelling a great distance through almost uninhabited country. One day he was warned, he stated, by unseen intelligence, that if he did not look properly to his buggy-shafts he would have an accident. Obeying the advice so far, he made a special examination of the shafts, and was astonished to discover they were unsafe. He then set to repair them, and had scarcely completed a part of the work when he was called away by his wife. "Something told" him, said he, that the work was not finished, and that he must return to it. His attention being, however, fully occupied with other things, he started on a journey without recollecting any-thing further about his shafts. After proceeding some dis-tance, the shafts gave way at a critical part of the road, and his horse becoming affrighted bolted. The buggy was smashed, and he was dragged some distance and severely injured. As he did not arrive at the place and time ex-pected, inquiries were set on foot and diligent search made along the road. The horse and parts of the buggy were discovered, and there were evidences of a disaster along the road otherwise, but his own whereabouts could not be found for some time. At last a friendly farmer who joined in the search was, as he himself had avowed to this minister, "led by God" to go to a small building at a distance which he knew to be deserted and closed up. On arriving at this place, he could see no signs of any one having been there. He tried the door, but found it securely fastened from within by strong pieces of wood. The only other aperture to the house was a window, and this too, on examination, was found to be securely fastened; but, on looking inside, he saw on the floor immediately under this window something covered over in an extraordinary manner. He also saw that a very small piece of the glass in one of the panes had been cut out, in size about as large as a threepenny piece, and per-fectly round and clean. He then forced the window, and there discovered my friend, who, in a very badly injured condition had been, in the absence of material beings to care for him, nursed by his guardian angels, the invisible messengers of God. How he had been transported and had gained entrance never could be cleared up, as the house bore no evidence of having been opened forcibly or otherwise previous to the farmer's discovery. His body was reposing on straw. His head was supported in such a way as to bring that portion of it which was most injured close up to and immediately under the little hole cut in the pane of the window. His body was covered with a mysteriously-woven cover of straw; and the wounded part of the head was also covered except in the centre or most injured spot, where there was a little opening, which was neatly worked around, forming a hole which corresponded in size with the hole in the pane of glass. He remembers being in great pain, and moaning from it, when a voice was heard to say, "Don't stir, you are being cared for." He then felt a cold current applied to the wounded part, as if a jet of cold water was being directed against one particular spot. He got relief almost immediately from that, and swooned over. Awaking again, he groaned from intense pain, and again a voice was heard to say, "You are getting better, don't stir;" and again he experienced the cold current, got relief, and swooned over. This statement is substantially true in its relation at second hand, for I can remember his account of it most clearly, although, of course, it is not pretended to be given in the exact words of his narrative.

During a visit to Melbourne, Australia, of Mr. Forster, the distinguished American medium, about three years since, I had a private sitting with him. Previous to calling upon him I had written several questions upon small strips of paper, separately, which strips were carefully folded up in such a manner as to hide the writing from view. After being so folded, they had all the same outward appearance, and there was nothing to distinguish one paper from another. They were all mixed up together, previous to being presented, so that as each was presented in its folded condition to Mr. Forster, neither he nor myself could, under ordinary circumstances,—that is, by the exercise of our eyesight,—distinguish or know what was the particular question written upon the inside. Nevertheless, as each strip so folded was handed to him, without opening it he placed it against his forehead and immediately thereupon gave, orally, to me an answer. Notes of those answers were taken at the time, and when they were placed alongside of the questions on the strips they referred to, they were found to be perfectly intelligent. Having been requested to write the names of three deceased friends or acquaintances upon strips in the same way folded and obscured from view, he placed these also upon his forehead; and, although merely the initials were written, he gave the full names of each and gave a characteristic message from each, which revealed the peculiarities of each as they were known to me in a marked manner, although the people named were private friends and relations quite unknown to the medium. After giving the name of a deceased brother, with a message from him, the medium turned up a sleeve of his coat, and, unbuttoning a wristband of his shirt, he uncovered his naked arm and showed to me plainly written thereon the name of my brother. For some time previous to visiting Mr. Forster, I had been receiving inspirational or impressional writing, and had passed through the lower phases of mediumship; and, amongst my other tests of Mr. Forster, one of the questions put to him was, whether I was mediumistic. He had no opportunity of conversing with me, nor of otherwise knowing who I was, for I called as a perfect stranger to him; yet, in answer to that question, he said, I was "a medium suited for the higher phases of inspiration." Some persons may argue that the reply given to the question of mediumship is not evidence in itself—that the knowledge he had gained of me in that respect was got through his clairvoyant powers, or that he obtained it from the spirit-world, as the science of phrenology teaches who are mediumistic by the mere outward form of the head. Professor Fowler, the phrenologist, for instance, had never seen me before, and I had not been many minutes in his rooms in London before he had arrived, through his knowledge of phrenology, at exactly the same conclusion. Within five minutes from the time I had presented myself at his rooms his hands had sufficiently explored my cranium to enable him to say, amongst other things, that I had "Spirituality" "full;" and the meaning which he gives of those two words on page 123 of his new illustrated "Self Instructor in Phrenology and Physiology," is thus rendered :

"Have a full share of high, pure, and spiritual feeling ; many premonitions or interior warnings and guidings, which, implicitly followed, conduct to success and happiness through life ; and an inner test or touchstone of truth, right, &c., in a kind of interior consciousness, which is independent of reason, yet, unperverted, in harmony with it ; are quite spiritual-minded, and, as it were, ' led by the Spirit.' "

Although it is obvious from this that such a knowledge of character may be gained through phrenology, it is also conclusive from the evidence of phrenologists that, with a certain development of the organ of " Spirituality," Mr. Forster, or any other medium, without necessarily being phrenologists, may obtain a true knowledge of character, as well as a true knowledge of many other matters. For, according to Professor Fowler, a " large " development of " Spirituality " means that such people—

" Perceive and know things independent of the senses or intellect, or, as it were, by prophetic intuition ; experience an internal consciousness of what is best, and that spiritual communion which constitutes the essence of true piety ; love to meditate ; experience a species of waking clairvoyance, as it were, forewarned, combined with large ' Veneration,' hold intimate communion with the Deity, who is profoundly adored ; and take a world of pleasure in that calm, happy, half-ecstatic state of mind caused by this faculty ; with large ' Causality,' perceive truth by intuition, which philosophical tests prove correct ; with large ' Comparison ' added, have a deep and clear insight into spiritual subjects, and embody a vast amount of the highest order of truth ; and clearly perceive and fully realise a spiritual state of being after death."

In the foregoing concise quotation taken from page 123 of his little book, the physiological principles that I have contended for are clearly upheld from a scientific point of view by a gentleman at the top of his profession, and of very large experience, so that the deductions so far of spirituality and of science are in harmony. Indeed, I am convinced that true inspiration suited to the spiritual requirements of any age—if devoutly sought after—will always be found in advance of the most profound scientific discoveries of that age, and will never be at variance with discovery ; hence, there is nothing to fear from research, except the discovery and correction of error, with all its attendant evils and despotic distortions ; and, as error is held to be the first condition of " sin," it follows that the true corrective or antidote is to be found in enlightenment.

He who really wishes to live in the Will of the Father, will try to do the greatest good to his fellow-creatures, and, in order to do this, he must gain a knowledge of their wants ; or, in a word, from a pure love of God, he must search out and become enlightened as to the laws of nature. John vii. : " My doctrine is not mine, but His that sent me. If any man will do His will, he shall know of the doctrine, whether it be of God, or whether I speak of myself." As want and supply, or desire and gratification, in the body and mind of man, the lower animals and plants, are held to be only another phase of the laws of attraction and repulsion under which the whole universe is supposed to be governed ; as healthy exercise brings strength, vigour, and development in mind and muscle ; and, as affinity grows out of contact, so does my experience of phrenology lead me to have confidence in it, and to believe that, if a man takes the trouble to find out the weak points of his own nature and habits, and desires spiritual aid for improvement, and exercises his best efforts in that direction, he will attract Divine mind-assistance, and his material organism will, in due time, conform to an improving condition of mind just as certain as if, by wilfully following a vicious course, his passions would grow stronger, and his material organism would conform more and more to his low course of life. At one time I was sceptical of phrenology. In youth, while in America, I got my head examined by a phrenologist, and his delineation agreed very closely with the following characters obtained from Mr. Hamilton in Australia. In 1856, having visited Melbourne, I called on Mr. Hamilton as a stranger, and he, having felt my bumps, wrote the following:

"This is a very nervous, active, excitable, and independent mind. His constitution is remarkably active, and his brain is ever earnest, and urged forward by warm feelings, strong passions, and a thirst for improvement. He is decidedly a friendly and companionable man, but he is refined in his tastes and in his habits, and has a love of intellectual conversation and respectable society. His appetites are temperate, and his sentiments disposed to cultivation and embellishment. He should take rest and not excite himself too much, as he is too nervous and too anxious. He is combative yet cautious, energetic yet rather depressed in ' Hope.' Not proud nor conceited, but respectful and discreet ; not vain, yet has a proper regard to good opinion. Very sensitive, and has Benevolence and also social sympathy in a high degree. He is fond of the sublime and beautiful. His taste for music, eloquence, and poetry is marked. Good reasoning powers and good language; could acquire languages well. Has a scientific head and fine mechanical talent. There is a tinge of melancholy in his nature."

Mr. Hamilton, about a year after this, paid a professional visit to the town I was then residing in, and as he had not kept any copy himself of the above-written character which he had given to me, I was very anxious to see whether in a second delineation by him there would be a close correspondence with the first ; accordingly, I called upon him again, and after my stating to him the test he was about to be subjected to, he cordially acquiesced, manipulated my head again and then wrote the following :—

"This is decidedly an intellectual head, and the temperament is of the most nervous kind; hence this gentleman must manifest much intellectual activity and fine sensibility. He has deep and powerful feelings, and will treat women and children with love and tenderness. He feels keenly, and has strong attachments. There is a tinge of melancholy in his nature from deep feeling and depressed 'Hope.' He is decidedly reflective and meditative, and inclined to the study of literature and moral science. He has scarcely enough of 'Self-esteem ;' and, as 'Cautiousness' and 'Love of Approbation' are large, he is shy and in some circumstances timid, at the same time he is combative and independent, and will think and act for himself. He has firmness of principle, though too cautious. He should endeavour to place himself in circumstances which would afford him opportunities of reading and study. He could acquire languages well, and reason with logical clearness. His perceptive powers are not so large as his reflective. 'Colour' seems only very moderate. 'Order' is active. Memory for technical terms only moderate. 'Imitation' large. His moral and intellectual powers have the predominance, though his feelings are strong. Cultivate 'Hope' and 'Self-esteem.' Very sensitive to the tender and the sublime in music, but the organs do not seem to have had full cultivation. Temperate in appetite, and regular in habits, yet very sensitive in mind. Critical and inquiring, and ever seeking knowledge."

In the year 1875, or eighteen years after Mr. Hamilton had written the above two characters, which correspond under the circumstances so closely to each other, Professor Fowler, of London, pronounced as follows on my head :—

"His tendencies to action are greater than those to rest. One of his leading features is power to persevere in times of trial, and to hold himself tenaciously to one course of life; but he could devote himself to subjects of an entirely new nature and throw his spirit into them. There must have been times when he had manifested unusual decision, determination, and presence of mind in times of danger. Another quality of mind arises from his desire to know the reason for everything, giving him power to think, plan, lay out work, to use judgment in matters of a complicated nature, and to be thorough in his investigations. He enjoys company when he can learn something or do something extra, but to go for mere social purposes would be a task. Another quality of his mind is energy, giving spirit, resolution, general efficiency, and industry. He is prepared to resist, to overcome, and defend, but does not appear to have much of the feelings of cruelty or revenge. 'Cautiousness,' too, in his case tends to give general prudence and forethought more than fear and timidity, and this, joined to conscience and firmness, has a powerful influence by way of giving consistency to his character, and disposes him to live a uniform life and to preach and practise the same doctrine. Conscience leads him to study himself and his own motives more than to find fault with others. He is reverential, has regard for sacred things, not naturally a scoffer or trifler with religious subjects, but not necessarily enthusiastic in religion, but 'Veneration' is so prominent he must have a regard for higher power than man. 'Benevolence' leads him to help persons in real want more than to aid where uncontrolled sympathy might instigate. He can regulate his sympathies better than 99 out of 100. He has much scope of mind, and takes the whole field of action into account; is generally thorough in what he takes hold of. He is not much of a talker, 'only talks when he has something to say,' and more frequently stops before he gets through than multiply words on the subject. He should be characterised for order, system, method, and accuracy in his mode of doing things, and is more orderly in his life and habits than most persons are. He is noted for a sense of punctuality, has no time to waste, and is mindful of the time of others, and tries to make the most of his time. He is a lover of nature, fine landscapes, flowers, colours, ornaments, beautiful and perfect things, and he is continually looking for something perfect, and is not satisfied with anything shoddy, but likes the pure article. He is quick to see the motives of others, and shrewd in perceiving the state of mind of a stranger. He is not cunning and artful, and could not succeed in a business where he had to be adroit or mysterious. He might follow a wholesale mercantile business, or something purely intellectual or scientific or artistic, but is not adapted for behind the counter, or to speak, or be a diplomatist where tact and worldly wisdom are required. He is not greedy for property, and is not proud nor domineering in spirit, but inclined to politeness, affability, and ease of manner.

The organ of 'Conscientiousness' is large. His 'Veneration' and Causality' are large, and his 'Benevolence' full. 'Self-esteem' is average. 'Firmness' is very large, and 'Cautiousness' is large. 'Secretiveness' only moderate. 'Hope' is full, and his 'Spirituality' is full."

A careful study of these three delineations of character, written at different times and referring to the same head, led to the conclusions,—1st, That the exercise of a sincere desire had attracted supply; 2d, That supply was of gradual growth; 3d, That by phrenology and physiology it can be demonstrated to our senses that, by the laws of God in nature, we have the shaping of our own characters, and to a great extent the shaping of the characters of our progeny in our own hands. It speaks well for the degree of perfection which has been reached in the science of phrenology by its professors, to find the remarkable correspondence in the nature of sketches given by different professors upon the same cast of head. It speaks well also for the science itself as such, to find from reasonable testimony that the functions of the brain are not only ascertained with exactness, but that experienced men have it in their power to do great and substantial good to humanity, for they can advise people as to which of their organs or points in their character they are most deficient in. With a knowledge of this kind, not only may young people with advantage be educated and brought up to businesses which they may reasonably be expected to excel in; but every one, if he so desires, has it within his own power to cultivate a good brain-organism, and with care in selecting a partner, he may transmit an improved class of organism, both mentally and physically, to his progeny, and thus perform a duty which perhaps more than any other is important, although it is the most shamefully neglected in these times of boasted civilisation and learning. On examination of the three delineations, there will be observed a marked difference in the condition of "Hope," "Language," "Music," mechanical ability, "Self-esteem," "Colour," and "Imitativeness," as reported by Mr. Hamilton and Mr. Fowler; but these differences furnish to me very powerful evidence that the brain-organs will grow with cultivation, use, or exercise, and get smaller with comparative disuse. In my case, this is notably so with the growth of "Hope." The depression of revengeful feeling, and the power of exercising benevolence˜ with greater discrimination. I had been brought up strictly to the religious forms and beliefs of the Presbyterian Church of Scotland, and attended Sunday-school twice, and church twice every Sunday, besides weekly Bible meetings. Notwithstanding all this training, I could never realise that " Christ " was God ; and, although I admired his teachings, I could not believe that I was doomed from birth because of Adam's supposed eating of certain fruit, and that it was only by Jesus' blood that I could be saved. As a boy, I could not reconcile the received attributes of God as being a Spirit infinite in wisdom and power, with the necessity for His resting after the six days of creation—with His having made man, who was to be subjected to a temptation which—it must have been known beforehand—he could not resist—with the justice of punishment inflicted upon man under such circumstances, and more especially upon his children, who had nothing to do with Eden—with the idea that He should have repented that He had made man— and with a host of other absurdities. I was quite willing to believe in the Fatherhood of God, and the brotherhood of mankind, and to regard God as an all-pervading spiritual intelligence of infinite wisdom and goodness ; but the theory of original sin, and the theory of modern redemption based upon that sin, baffled all my powers of logical deduction. As a boy, battling these difficulties in my mind, I remember kneeling in earnest prayer in my room, and asking earnestly for light as to whether these things were true, and I recollect arising from my knees fully impressed they were not literally true. Yet still a doubt had been deeply implanted in me by those incessant teachings, and they threw a melancholy and doubt over my mind because I could not be clear. Some years ago, however, I began to inquire earnestly and honestly into spiritism and its higher teachings, and these brought the light I wanted. I could see a reason, and realise a religion, for myself ; and from that time I became a hopeful, and I may say a happy man —one who in heart could exclaim, Death, where is thy sting ? or Grave, thy victory ? I could then better understand how it was that as we sow we reap, and the teachings of God, through nature and the inward monitor, have taken the place of the pulpit preacher ; and, by the exercise of an earnest desire, there has been attracted the spiritual mind-assistance sought; and my head has in time been got more into shape, as a consequence, and the phrenologist can observe the increased development of " Hope " and " Veneration." With me, the observed loss in " Language," " Music," and mechanical development may as easily be accounted for, therefore, in the fact that these faculties had not been much exercised, and hence they figured relatively less prominent in the report of Mr. Fowler than in the earlier delineations of Mr. Hamilton.

Mr. Gladstone, on the occasion of a recent distribution of prizes among students in the Schools of Science, in alluding to the city companies, said they were founded for the purpose of developing their arts and trades, and to make the processes of their industry at once beautiful, economical, and effective; and, as an illustration of what might be done towards an improvement in the designs, and the greater beauty of the workmanship, by systematic efforts towards the entertwining of beauty with utility, he said :

" I remember the time when I began life as a young man, you were laughed at if you declared that the human being, as such, was musical. You were considered a fool, a dreamer, an enthusiast. People used to say, ' I cannot tell one note from another.' I used to reply, ' If your nurse, who carried you when you were six months old, had continued to carry you until you were forty years old, as you are now, would you have been able to walk ? ' I believe that faculties uncultivated die within. The human mind has within itself capability to call out the faculties that are inborn ; and if labour is applied these faculties will be developed, and those who have had the sense to make this use of them will find they augment largely the enjoyments of human nature."

The teachings of phrenology go to establish the views advanced in the earlier part of this work—namely, that it is only when a person naturally feels the " want " of the divine spirit (that heavenly food wherewith to satisfy the cravings of his higher nature, to bring to him a happiness beyond that of the mere gratification of the material desires), that his mind or soul can expect to draw or attract spiritual happiness. The ripening of mind for a higher condition of existence than that represented in our material bodies must be gradual, and in accordance with certain observed laws. In other words, while "conversion" may be a sudden experience, or a bursting forth into existence of a want not before fully realised, "reform and godly character" is a matter of time, and must grow naturally out of the exercise of pure earnest desire.

It is really marvellous how beautiful, ennobling, and hopeful are the laws of pure natural religion, and how readily they may be understood by reason of their simplicity when they are stripped of the mysterious trappings of theology, and relieved from those tyrannical links with which priestcraft and tradition have, with such unutterable cruelty and ignorance, striven to keep the mind of man enslaved. It is not that the teachers of religion deny such a thing as prayer and communion with God, but it is the way in which they administer teachings on these vital high-roads to human elevation. At a time when the world of mind is thirsting to the death for the nearest road in which to seek a loving Father, these "blind leaders of the blind" are trying to lead it every way but in a right straightforward way. If the people of the New Testament had been no further advanced in mind, they would have been left under the ceremonial laws of Moses, and they would not have required such a teacher as Jesus of Nazareth amongst them, to teach them that henceforth, instead of an eye for an eye and a tooth for a tooth, they should, if smitten on one cheek, turn the other also to the smiter. No minister of pure religion understood as well as Jesus the necessity of administering to mind according to its growth and requirements. John, 4th chapter : "Say not ye, There are yet four months, and then cometh harvest. Behold I say unto you, Lift up your eyes and look on the fields ; for they are white already to harvest." He spoke of the condition of mind being such that it was ripening for an ingathering, and not of the crops which were not nearly ripe. At that same time, he treated of the subject of prayer thus: "Believe me, the hour cometh when ye shall neither in this mountain, nor yet at Jerusalem, worship the Father. . . . The hour cometh, and now is, when the true worshippers shall worship the Father in spirit and in truth ; for the Father seeketh such to worship him. God is a Spirit: and they that worship Him must worship Him in spirit and in truth." In trying to follow the ruling laws of nature as they present themselves under different aspects, according to the stages of existence in which they operate, whether in the grosser material nature or in the sublimate spiritual state, it was sought to identify the laws of desire, want, and supply with the laws of affinity and growth, and the universal laws of attraction and repulsion, whether in magnetism, motion, heat, combustion, colour, or power,—all of these being exercised by mind. In alluding to phrenology and the power which people are endowed with, of improving their natures through the exercise of a sincere desire to do so,—the desire of the mind, attracting from the God-mind the power of reform, and the material nature or organism conforming, accordingly, in its growth to such mind-exercise,—there is furnished to the reader a pretty clear idea of how the law of prayer operates. Who has not felt, at some period or other of his life, the power of prayer, or, in other words, the power obtained through the exercise of a pure spiritual desire for good? I have no hesitation in giving my testimony that, without any doubt in my mind, I have received at times spiritual mind-power in answer to prayer, which has sufficed to enable me to overcome evil desires which I had before found myself unequal to grapple with, and which had given me much trouble on that account. The parable of the importunate woman illustrates the action of the law by which, through constant, earnest, pure desire, we may attract spiritual assistance and answers to prayers. But the people of our day have not had it made plain to their advanced comprehensions how prayer acts. They are as tenacious of tradition as they were when Jesus spoke to the woman at the well; and while some will insist that their particular "mountain" or their "Jerusalem" is the only correct place to pray, others insist that prayer is only a form, and that an unknown language is the correct thing to use. Let ministers make a study of those laws of God in nature which govern the operation of mind, and, instead of wasting useful time on Sundays by uttering solemn platitudes, let them expound the science of prayer and of true religion, and bring people to understand and practise, and feel a hope and happiness in what they profess.

Having related my experiences in phrenology and prayer, and how they support the conclusions arrived at in the former part of this work, I purpose here to relate another phase of experience in mediumship.   After developing sufficiently to receive *verbatim* inspirational writing, I abandoned, as before stated, the use of the lower form of mediumship known as "mechanical writing," and soon lost, as a consequence, the power of receiving legible writing by that means.   About this time I was "impressed" to undertake a lengthy journey, and, as it involved very serious considerations, I was anxious to prove the correctness of the impression, when a new test-channel was unexpectedly opened to me in the following way :—My wife, although anxious to obtain " mechanical writing" for some time, had not succeeded in her endeavours while sitting for it, beyond obtaining a slight movement of her hand, but no writing.   One evening, after thinking of her anxiety to become a "mechanical writer," we sat together with pencil and paper before us, and it occurred to me that by uniting hands, although neither of us could write, we might succeed. Accordingly, having commenced by making a few magnetic passes down her right arm, I placed my right hand sufficiently over hers to touch it without applying enough muscular power to move it, and it was found to our astonishment that by this means, she was constituted a first-rate " mechanical writing medium."   It was found that, while both of us (blindfolded, and with our heads turned away from the paper before us, allowed our hands in such union to be moved), could exercise our minds, and keep up a conversation upon subjects having no reference whatever to the writing received, in this way we could receive written communications, in another style of handwriting, which were easily read after their conclusion.   Much good advice was given to us in these messages, and, amongst other matters, I received a clear confirmation of my "impression" to go on that journey ; and such was the confidence reposed in that confirmation and test, that preparations were forthwith made, and the journey, which extended over a distance of about forty-three thousands of miles, was undertaken and accomplished with satisfactory results.   Having, in my earlier experiences and inquiries, seen sufficient evidence of the exercise of an unexplained power by unseen intelligence, my inclinations did not lead me much to follow up what is called the " physical phenomena " of spiritism ; recently, however, during a short sojourn in London, I was present at a sitting for physical manifestations. I got into the room before the sitters arrived, and made a thorough careful examination of every part of it with a good light. The floor under the carpet, the doors with their panels and locks were looked to, the ceiling and walls were sounded and examined, as well as all the things in the room carefully overhauled by me, and I was satisfied that no stage illusions were used, and waited in the room until the sitters arrived. Scarcely had the doors been secured, and the hands of every one present joined, than several articles were moved about the room, although it was obvious that none of the sitters were moving them. A chair, with a large musical-box upon it, which weighed about 15 lbs., was drawn or moved from a far corner of the room, out of the reach of any sitter, and brought close up to the medium, and although both his hands were being held at the time, his left arm was found to be unlinked with or passed through the open back of the chair. A guitar was floated about our heads, its strings being sounded the while, and other things also seemed to be moved, and were moved, while the sitters remained at the table; but as these things were done in the dark, we had not, of course, the evidence of our eyesight. To any one that had not, like myself, witnessed the exercise of an unexplained power by unseen intelligence in broad day-light and in gas-light, of course he might still remain unsatisfied that such things were possible. The chair being placed on the arm of a person whose hand is being held, involves the phenomenon of the passage of matter through matter. The explanation given of this process is, that matter is held together by a certain power according to its nature; and that, by the envelopment of the most fragile article within an invisible sphere, propelled with such a force, or at such a velocity, as to be more than sufficient to overcome the power of cohesion of the material to be penetrated, such article may be carried through such material in such a way as not to show the direction of its passage, and at the same time to be uninjured in its transit. Man has not arrived at such a state of discovery yet as to enable him to apply this process. He can send a message under the waters of the Atlantic across to America from England, however, and that would have been considered, a few years ago, quite as impossible as sending an egg through a stone

M

wall may be considered, until we know how it can be done. It is said a man may shoot a tallow candle through the panel of a door, and, perhaps, with a little ingenuity he might catch the candle uninjured after passing through the door ; but his ingenuity does not, up to this time, enable him to hide the hole made by its passage through the door. Yet, electricity passes through any conductor without revealing its course of passage to our eyesight. "There are," verily, "more things in heaven and earth than are ever dreamt of in our philosophy,"—and the things which are now revealed to us are not all that can be revealed, but only such as may suffice to awaken inquiry in the mind of man. A neighbour of mine is an extraordinary powerful "physical medium." I have never witnessed any of the manifestations in her presence, but am personally acquainted with a highly cultivated and trustworthy lady, who has been an earnest inquirer for truth for many years, and has publicly borne evidence of the nature of manifestations which she herself, in company with several others (all of whom are to the fore), did witness in the presence of this medium. A common soup-plate, containing twenty eggs, was, during a sitting of these persons with closed doors, conveyed from the medium's own locked-up residence a distance of nearly two miles, to where she was then in the company of these sitters, and it was placed on the table in the midst of them without noise. Upon another occasion, at the same place with some other sitters and this same medium, a cup of tea was brought from her house, and other articles from other parts were also brought to them. Evidence may readily be obtained of the levation of people, and even the materialisation of spirit-forms, but I prefer to confine myself to phenomena within my own experience, and as such manifestations have not been sought after there has been no necessity to witness them, otherwise, no doubt, I might have witnessed them. If people believe in their Bibles throughout, however, they are forced to believe that such things are possible. John xx. : When Mary went to the sepulchre for the body of Jesus and saw the two angels and questioned them, she turned back "and saw Jesus standing." He said, "Woman, why weepest thou? whom seekest thou?" and, on her answering he said, "Mary, touch me not, for I am not yet ascended to my Father, but go to my brethren and say unto them, I ascend unto my Father, and unto your Father, and to my God and your God." The evening of the same day, "when the doors were shut where the disciples were assembled for fear of the Jews, came Jesus and stood in the midst, and saith unto them, Peace be unto you." Thomas was not present at the time, and when he was told of it, said he would not believe "except I shall see in his hands the print of the nails, and put my finger into the print of the nails, and thrust my hand into his side." After eight days, the disciples were again gathered and Thomas was this time present. "Then came Jesus, the doors being shut, and stood in their midst, and said, Peace be unto you. Then saith he to Thomas, Reach hither thy finger, and behold my hands; and reach hither thy hand, and thrust it into my side : and be not faithless." After this Jesus showed himself again to the disciples at the Sea of Tiberias as they were fishing, and on their coming to shore he took bread and gave to them, and fish likewise; and after they had dined, it was that Jesus said to "Simon Peter," "Lovest thou me more than these?" For it was at Peter's proposal the disciples had gone fishing, that being Peter's original occupation, and he thereby evincing a disposition to return to it now that Jesus had been sacrificed, instead of following the ministry. Peter answered, "Yea, Lord, thou knowest that I love thee," and Jesus responded, "Feed my lambs." It was evident that Peter did not fully comprehend or appreciate the depth of the proposition put, the real nature of which was not as to whether he had a kindly feeling towards Jesus, but whether he sympathised sufficiently with Jesus' mission of at-one-ment, to desert for ever the worldly employment to which he was again turning attention, and devote himself entirely to the work of God by feeding the lambs and sheep of Jesus' fold with that spiritual nourishment which he had received on trust through Jesus, and which consisted of those high and lofty teachings which were intended to raise and ennoble the whole world of mind. As Peter could not fully see the question in that light, it was put to him three times, and each time with the injunction to feed the sheep and lambs, and these repeated questions and injunctions evidently had the desired effect of awakening Peter's mind to a full comprehension of his mission, for, as was predicted of him, he died in harness. The 8th chapter of Acts relates of Philip being told of the angel of the Lord to go toward the south unto Gaza ; that he went, and, seeing a man of authority in a chariot reading Esaias, the Spirit said, "Go near and join thyself to this chariot." Philip did so, and was asked to explain the Scripture, and having done so, "the Spirit of the Lord caught away Philip" that the man of authority saw him no more, "but Philip was found at Azotus." It would be altogether too lengthy a task to attempt to quote the instances related in Scripture, both in the Old and New Testaments, of the occurrence of spiritual phenomena such as have been here related, and it is a position which no one can gainsay, that if they are believed in the one case, there is no sufficient reason to show why they should not be believed in the other, more especially as primary evidence of present phenomena may be obtained by any one who has any real desire to witness them. I know of two instances in Australia where individuals have been raised off the ground ; but, as mention has previously been made of heavy articles having been lifted and removed in my presence in the light, there does not appear to be any reason why people as well as inanimate things should not be moved by this same power. To me, therefore, the statement that a Mr. Home or a Mrs. Guppy were raised and carried by such unseen and unexplained force is not beyond belief, altogether irrespective of Scripture testimony. With reference to visions, it may be here stated that I have frequently experienced them in sleep, seeing people and places both known and unknown, and that I have seen mansions, terraces, and flowers far surpassing in beauty anything that my experience or imagination could call to mind in wakeful times or under ordinary circumstances. A phase of mediumship, not known to be common, is experienced by me, in being able to distinguish the appearance and features of known and unknown faces, in close proximity to me, during the ordinary affairs of the day, in the light. These are not seen through the eyes, as if I were looking at an object, but their appearance is realised, as it were, through the brain direct. I am not in a position to explain how, under delirium tremens, people appear to see other people and things, never having so much as tasted spirituous liquors in all my life, but imagine it must be a somewhat different phenomenon to what is here alluded to. Of one thing I am satisfied, and that is, if people have a true desire for inquiry, they will soon realise the actuality of an after-state, the nearness of their departed friends, and the astonishing intimacy there is between things present and things future, things seen and things unseen. There are in my possession some memoranda of spirit travel, within my own experience, some particulars of which I shall here note. While on shipboard, on the South Pacific Ocean, in the year 1875, at 140° west of Greenwich, during sleep, I distinctly experienced that I was carried away in spirit to a place where my wife and children were, at 145° east of Greenwich, and that I there saw them in my house asleep. I called my wife, who is a heavy sleeper, by a familiar name, and she, awakening partially, replied, "Well! what is it?" I then said, "About ten days' sail from the Cape. All is going well. Good-bye." I experienced some difficulty in getting back again to my body, in consequence of the attraction of one of my children, which attraction had to be relaxed before I could return ; and I was unconscious during my return to the ship. Calculating the hours by the distance, my spirit must have been with my family at from twelve to one o'clock at midnight. In my first letter to my family I gave the particulars, and my wife declares that she remembers being awakened, under the circumstances indicated, about the time the "travel" was said to have occurred. Another singular circumstance may be worth relating. My wife had no knowledge of what time I would return from a voyage to England and America, as my originally expressed intention was to remain eighteen months. From an impression received while in America, I altered my intention quite suddenly, and returned by first steamer, arriving within eight months of my departure, and before my letter could have reported my altered plans. Yet she, at the Antipodes, seemed to know impressionally of the exact time I would return, for she mentioned the middle of November as the time she expected me to several persons, weeks before my return, which really did occur on 15th November. My oldest son, who was at college away from home, tells me that on the night of my return a footstep was heard on the floor of the verandah, and at the door of the college a knock. The servant attending the door found no signs of any one, and declared it to be a "ghost," and refused to answer it a second time. My brother's widow, living in another part of the country, assured me very seriously, so soon as she saw me, that my brother had appeared to her on the night of my arrival, and had pointed me out, arriving on the water in the port. A great number of little incidents of the kind might be mentioned, but as they are chiefly matters of more personal than public interest, they are withheld at the present time. With the knowledge, however, which has been revealed of matters having public importance, sufficient to establish the evidence advanced of the operation of laws by which Man may realise a clear and more loving connection with his Maker under a "natural religion," I feel the duty rests upon me of making these things known to others. The rain, after it has moistened the ground, is absorbed by the glowing heat of the sun, and is drawn up into the air to be distilled, to descend again in refreshing showers so soon as the earth has had enough of light and heat, and thirsts for it, or WANTS it again to fall. The planets receive light, and they reflect it out again, with more or less strength, according to the perfection of their condition and their atmosphere. So, then, do we find in nature that law of duty which teaches us that as we receive so should we give out. We find also there should be no individual ownership, as all things are on trust for use as they are sent; and as nothing can be exhausted, so should nothing be locked up and hoarded to satisfy the craving for selfish ownership, or the desire to gain power and advantage over our fellow-beings.

MEDIUMSHIP AND CIRCLES.

As some persons profess not to know anything of what revelation, inspiration, or impression is, or how it may be cultivated, it may not be unprofitable to say a few words under the heading selected, before closing this work. The reader—if he has any respect for himself—must admit that he knows something of what conscience is, and what prayer is. Well, the simple exercise of true prayer, or a desire for truth and to lead an improved life, conforming in all things to the will of God, with a willingness to receive His pure teachings, setting aside the erroneous God-dishonouring doctrines of sectarianship, society, and custom, will of itself cultivate mediumship, and bring revelation. It is worldly selfishness and wilfulness which keep people in darkness. Every thought and desire should be pure, and in all things our undertakings should be governed by that at-one-ment of purpose exemplified in those words of Jesus, "Yet not my will, but Thine be done." We should test the purity of all our plausible resolutions, promptings, and undertakings, by examining carefully whether "self" be in any way mixed up in them—and if it is, we should at once be suspicious of our own thoughts. A study of phrenology, and the experiences gained of results, go to establish the statement that a love of God, and the study of our own natures, with an earnest desire for improvement, is the best possible means of developing mediumship. When conscience has been disabused of erroneous teachings—and the desires and associations are uncontaminating, seek wisdom and spiritual food from the Father—the "Spirit of Truth"—and abide by and follow closely the revelations or impressions which may be received. There is only one "sin," said Jesus, which cannot be pardoned, that is, sin against the Holy Ghost, or in other words, the whisperings of a pure conscience, or the revelation given through the "Spirit of Truth." Whenever man acts against his conscientious convictions, he writes an entry to his debit in the book of his own soul which can never be blotted out, although the bitter memory of his fault may lead him to desire and receive that spiritual strength which may enable him to overcome another worldly fault of the same kind, and in that way do him good.

Spiritual Circles are formed differently for different objects. For instance, there are circles for cultivating IMPRESSIONAL writing, speaking, drawing, painting, and music, or for general or special educational purposes—there are circles also for getting MECHANICAL writing, drawing, music, &c. ; and there are circles for PHYSICAL manifestations of different kinds. Now, for all these circles to succeed, it is requisite that the members offering be specially suited, physically, for one or other of them. In the formation of circles, it is, therefore, most desirable first to ascertain for which particular circle each is best suited. The best mode of ascertaining this is, first to get them all seated at a table in circle with hands touching each other. Then to feel their hands, and those whose hands are most cold are best suited for the PHYSICAL manifestations — the next coldest for the MECHANICAL — and the warmest are best for IMPRESSIONAL. There is another way of proceeding, which is that, after getting all seated in circle, to ask the spiritual intelligence present to indicate by rapping or moving the table as to which person in the circle is the strongest medium, and that being done, he to ask the intelligence to rap out the mediumship for which each present is naturally best fitted ; thus, one rap to represent physical, two raps mechanical, and three raps impressional. The room should be a quiet, healthy room, not uncomfortably hot nor cold ; and not one that is used by many persons, as the magnetic influences, if possible, should not be mixed. Those present during the sitting should be careful to keep their hands touching each other, until a strong current of magnetism be established ; and there should be perfect earnestness, honesty of purpose, and quiet for about fifteen or twenty minutes. Soft slow music may be played with advantage during the sitting. If not successful the first time, the attempt should be persevered with at a given place, day, and hour, regularly every week until successful. In sitting, those present should be placed positive and negative, dark and fair complexions, or male and female alternately. There is no necessity for any particular number at any sitting; and family circles, or circles composed of from two to six persons associating much together, or otherwise in affinity, are invariably the most successful. The physical manifestations are sometimes most wonderful where only one good suitable medium for those particular phenomena is present; for, by means of a current of magnetism which can be worked in connection with such a medium, articles of considerable weight may be carried for a distance, and even through rooms with all their openings closed. For mechanical writing, &c., after a few sittings, a person whose arm and hand is moved readily, may develop his mediumship by sitting alone, but this should not be too often done, as it will occasion a disturbance of the nerve-current which will prove injurious. For inspirational or impressional writing, &c., persons are as well sitting alone, or, if in affinity, two or three may at same time sit quietly in a room, and they may even develop by desire, without sitting. It is most important that people should not sit for communications without their minds are in a pure train; and there should be no disturbing influences, bad magnetism, or bad associations about. Good impressional mediums are generally most sensitive to bad magnetism while in close contact with other persons; and they frequently suffer much inconvenience and even pain from such a cause without being very well able to obviate it —while under such circumstances, for instance, as that of travelling in crowded conveyances or sitting in large assemblages. They can, however, often relieve themselves afterwards by making rapid magnetic passes or strokes with their hands down their bodies from head to feet, thus brushing off any bad magnetism from their bodies and limbs. There are many other kinds of mediumship, such as Trance, which are not here alluded to. Sleep, too, is often chosen by our impressors as a favourable time for communicating with us in visions, in whisperings, and otherwise. I have known credible persons to lecture in public from spirit-voice promptings and dictation; while many people quite commonly obtain promptings, in matters of importance, from their spiritual guides by putting mental questions and receiving affirmative answers or encouragement by a nervous

twitching in the right hand and arm, or a singing in the right
ear, or receiving negative or deterrent answers by a twitching in the left arm, or a singing sensation in the left ear.
Although the phenomena under physical mediumship may
not appear very intellectual or improving, it must be borne
in mind that, like everything else, it has its uses, and it has
been a means by which many persons who had settled into
materialistic opinions (without belief in a spiritual state, or
the existence of mind after the decay of the body) have been
aroused to conviction by the evidences of spirit-power and
intelligence which these phenomena have afforded.   As for
the higher phases of mediumship, all religious teachings and
revelation are due to and grounded upon them ; and our
higher nature is built up altogether on their operations,
whether we can recognise the laws under which those operations are worked or not.   The sayings and teachings of Jesus
are full of spiritism, and they show that he had a very clear
knowledge of mediumship and phenomena.   In Matthew,
18th chapter, he is represented to have said : " If two of you
shall agree on earth as touching anything that they shall ask,
it shall be done for them of my Father."   " For where two
or three are gathered together in my name, there am I
in the midst of them."   Jesus believed himself to have a
special mission, which consisted in administering to ripening
mind the advanced truths which were to elevate and ennoble the human mind, to implant higher and purer conceptions of Deity, and to improve the morals and every-day life
of the people ; and that mission he zealously and faithfully
performed while in the body.   Such passages as those just
quoted show that by his deep spiritual insight, he traced
his mission beyond the mere material form of existence ;
and, through a desire still to minister to those whom he
should leave on this earth, he communicated to them the
conditions under which communion might be established
and kept up between those in the body with those in the
spirit.   In John, 14th and 15th chapters, after telling them
of his approaching dissolution, he shows them plainly that
it is his desire, after leaving the body, still to remain a
channel of pure spiritual truth and enlightenment.   " I am
the vine, ye are the branches."   " If ye abide in me and my
words abide in you, ye shall ask what ye will, and it shall
be done unto you.   Herein is my Father glorified, that ye

bear much fruit." " These things have I spoken unto you that my joy might remain in you, and that your joy might be full." Any person having a knowledge of spiritism, and labouring with others in the will of the Father for the general good, may well express himself in those words, and desire to retain the affection and affinity, after death, of his fellow-labourers, in order that he may from his higher sphere of observation continue his assistance in such good work. Persons sitting, especially for the more ennobling phenomena of inspiration, should invariably centre their minds and exercise a strong desire for Divine impression ; for, while such desire tends to repulse low influences (always eager to communicate), it will not repulse pure-minded departed friends who may be able and willing to lead us to truth and happiness, and whose every wish may be to live in harmony with nature, studying in all things conformity with the will of God. To such, however, as have no sincere desire for spiritual light and improvement, any investigation of spiritual phenomena or revelation through any channel, will have little effect, as an earnest desire for improvement must precede reform. " If they hear not Moses and the prophets, neither will they be persuaded though one rose from the dead." ·

THE END.

PRINTED BY BALLANTYNE, HANSON AND CO.
EDINBURGH AND LONDON

Check Out More Titles From HardPress Classics Series In this collection we are offering thousands of classic and hard to find books. This series spans a vast array of subjects – so you are bound to find something of interest to enjoy reading and learning about.

Subjects:
Architecture
Art
Biography & Autobiography
Body, Mind &Spirit
Children & Young Adult
Dramas
Education
Fiction
History
Language Arts & Disciplines
Law
Literary Collections
Music
Poetry
Psychology
Science
…and many more.

Visit us at www.hardpress.net

Im TheStory

personalised classic books

"Beautiful gift.. lovely finish.
My Niece loves it, so precious!"

Helen R Brumfieldon

★★★★★

UNIQUE
GIFT

FOR KIDS, PARTNERS
AND FRIENDS

Timeless books such as:

Kids

Alice in Wonderland • The Jungle Book • The Wonderful Wizard of Oz
Peter and Wendy • Robin Hood • The Prince and The Pauper
The Railway Children • Treasure Island • A Christmas Carol

Adults

Romeo and Juliet • Dracula

Highly
Customizable

Change
Books Title

Replace
Characters Names
with yours

Upload
Photo that
appear page

Add
Inscriptions

Visit
Im TheStory .com
and order yours today!